# THE UNBREAKABLE MARRIAGE:

# 20 COMMANDS OF MARRIAGE

**DR. JERMAEL AND DR. CARRIE ANTHONY**

The Unbreakable Marriage:
20 Commands of Marriage

Published 2021 by Kingdom at Hand International Ministries

Content in the Unbreakable Marriage: 20 Commands of Marriage is taken from The Four Laws of Love: Guaranteed Success for Every Marriage Couple, © 2019 by Jimmy Evans.

Unless otherwise noted, all Scripture quotations are taken from the King James Version of the Bible.

Scripture quotations marked AMP are from the Amplified Bible. Copyright © 2015 by The Lockman Foundation,
La Habra, CA 90631. All rights reserved.

Scripture quotations marked ESV are from the English Standard Version. The Holy Bible, English Standard Version. ESV® Text Edition: 2016. Copyright © 2001 by Crossway Bibles, a publishing ministry of Good News Publishers.

Cover Design by: Graphic Maker 00
Edited by: Heaven and Earth Unite, LLC
Book Layout by: Heaven and Earth Unite, LLC
heunite@gmail.com


Paperback ISBN: 978-1-7367964-0-5
E-book ISBN: 978-1-7367964-1-2
Audio Book: 978-1-7367964-2-9

# TABLE OF CONTENTS

## DR. JERMAEL & DR. CARRIE'S UNBREAKABLE BONUS

# ACKNOWLEDGEMENTS

To my Lord and Savior: Thank You. We love You forever and eternity. We appreciate You. All strange gods stand last to You. You have resurrected You, Your marriage, family and ministry. We are indebted and fully grateful. You have carried You and we are FULLY persuaded in You, forever.

To Our parents: Darrell and Myrtis Betton, (Late) William and Malikah Daniels and Jerry and (Late) Lee Anthony, thank You for the lessons of healthy marriage, teaching You from childhood and in adult conversation the importance of Jesus, marriage and family! We love and appreciate You!

To Our children: Josiah Lovelace, Kai Ariana, and Myah Reign, we love you and want you to learn about healthy marriage and family life. Take these lessons with you into adulthood to have lasting marriages with Christ Jesus at the foundation.

To Apostle and Elder Malone, Apostle and Pastor Stovall, Archbishop and Pastor Isaac, and Apostle and Pastor Jacobs, thank you for your stance in the body of Christ! May the Lord bless you, your families, legacies, and ministries in abundance.

To Kingdom at Hand International Ministries and Tapley Nation: Many Blessings. May we all ascend in health, wealth, time, and increase in stature together in Christ! We love each of you deeply!

# PREFACE

The Unbreakable Marriage was birthed through a series of labor and deliveries within our marriage. The concept did not come into fruition until understood our deliverance and healing and not just coping with dysfunction. During the deepest trauma of our pain we were taught how to contend for our marriage and the marriages of our fellow brothers and sisters in the body of Christ. We developed such sensitivity to those who have undergone the pain of disconnection of intimacy, misunderstandings, mismanagement of money and finances, loss, grief of adultery, and sexual traumas.

Our marital story began September 2005. We were young, broke, happy, serving Jesus, and madly in love. We dated as teenagers and met in middle school. We truly thought in our marriage infancy that marriage would be easy. Boy… were we mistaken! Marriage is hard work, and whatever you put in you will indeed get out! Whatever you sow you will reap! This is what marriage looks like. We did not always work for the affections of the other. We did not always study how to steward our finances well; and we did not always understand that Your sexuality would ultimately define You as individuals and in oneness inside our marriage. We did not always understand that communication is key, and nonverbal communication is as important as verbal communication.

We have had our share of knock-down-drag-out arguments where our environment was a complete warzone, and one spouse slept in the bed while the other remained on the couch in the den. We both were previously well acquainted with sexual trauma at the hands of older family members well before marriage and then inflicted that pain upon one another with hyper and hypo sexuality, pornography, masturbation, and even adultery. We were also well in touch with playing the roles of happy, healthy, and whole while we were unhappy, unhealthy, and broken while trapped within the demands of ministry, work, and extended family. Along with these demands, we were suffering in silence. We were threatening divorce and separation as an only option because we felt we did not have anywhere to turn for help.

People on the outside were enthralled with us playing a happy role! It spoke volumes to them of unspoken alliances with pain and misery. As a result, we felt like we could not try out others with our private failures. This lack of openness and accountability caused our character to go unchecked until Jesus came to set us free by exposing darkness and hidden secrets, secret lifestyles, and secret adulterous relationships, while peeling back the layers of who we really were without facades. Once we were introduced to each other and ourselves, brought into health by Archbishop Isaac, and then reintroduced to a Father who genuinely loves and cares deeply for us, then and only then did we come into happiness, wholeness, health, and truth within our marriage!

Inside of our marital journey, we learned that healthy and happy marriages are built, so we decided to invest in our marriage and attend marriage classes by Apostle and Elder Malone who instructed everyone on the precepts of marriage (the unspoken biblical laws of marriage). Once we took the notes and enacted what we learned, we began to live out the reality of a happy marriage without the anguish. We were officially comfortable in our marriage and could deal with and talk about anything. Do we argue? Yes. Do we get frustrated with one another? Yes. Are we perfect for one another? Yes. Do we understand that we are not deliberately inflicting pain and irritation upon one another? Yes. We are both so secure with who we are individually andcollectively that we can be whoever we are in the moment, and know without a doubt that no one is leaving, no one is cheating, and no one's opinion is changing about the other spouse. And, this is the comfort of investing in our marriage (building your marriage): we pray. God answers. We change accordingly. God provides the escape. We live, and God covers us together! By virtue of God's glory restoring our marriage, we want to see all marriages healed and restored. We know the good, bad, and ugly. We know healthy and unhealthy. Because of this grace God has given, we desire to see all marriages healthy and happy!

# Introduction

The Unbreakable Marriage (your firstborn in this marriage ministry) has been indeed written by both of us: Jermael and Carrie. Many assume Jermael wrote most of the book or assume Carrie wrote most of the book. However, we have come up with a pattern of writing to bring the book into our oneness of writing and communication. We both share in equity the writing of this work. In The Unbreakable Marriage, we streamline our words, phrases, and thoughts during our editing to give the exact same voice and authority. Only those who know us intimately can accurately identify who wrote what because they know how we think and how it flows from our spirit. In keeping this same spirit, we both are equally co-authoring the books. It is our goal for everyone who is desiring, considering, and are married to understand the laws, jurisdictions, investments, connections, roles, rules, and proximities within marriage to either affirm a steady road for healthy marriages or restore broken marriages. Moreover, it is also our goal that we reflect this authority of oneness in marriage within our writing. We will not relent until marriages in the body of Christ are embracing the wholeness of Jesus and the miraculous power of oneness!

*Set me as a seal upon thine heart,*
*as a seal upon thine arm:*
*for love is strong as death;*
*jealousy is cruel as the grave:*
*the coals thereof are coals of fire,*
*which hath a most vehement flame.*
*Many waters cannot quench love,*
*neither can the floods drown it:*
*if a man would give all the*
*substance of his house for love,*
*it would utterly be condemned.*

**SONGS OF SOLOMON 8:6-7**

# I

## Thou Shalt Prepare For Marriage

*Therefore, prepare your minds for action, keep sober in spirit, fix your hope completely on the grace to be brought to you at the revelation of Jesus Christ.*

**- I Peter 1:13 (NASB)**

The marriage journey definitely begins long before the wedding. Oftentimes, women as young girls idolize the "Big Wedding Day." Usually people do not give attention to the fact that the wedding ceremony (or going to Justice of the Peace) only lasts thirty minutes tops. And, even within those thirty minutes, the day of idolizing others in the reality of sharing life, space, money, food, bed, communication, body, children, prayer lives, and intermingling of extended families begins. The truth is that most are unprepared for real life and real issues that are invited in by saying, "I DO." The reality is that long before marriage you must prepare if it is desired! How do you prepare for marriage? This is how to prepare for marriage: read books, go to marriage seminars, join a marriage group at church, ask married friends questions about their life and truths, read scripture, and lean on the Holy Spirit for direction. For men, preparation looks like surrendering everything within to Christ Jesus, such as: lying, pornography, multiple women "friends," going to proper places to "create the opportunity to find a wife," and preparing the mind to be a special woman's husband and blessed child's father.

1

Pray! Men must pray. It teaches you how to cover your home! It also looks like gaining accountability partners to assist in keeping you healthy, holy, and accountable sexually, financially, and spiritually. Moreover, making sure that you are clean cut, well dressed, smelling good, and preparing your mind for commitment and love with one woman alone is preparing for marriage. A woman's preparation also means carrying oneself as a wife. Wifehood is an anointing. Keeping your body in the spirit of holiness (inside and outside), dressing up, keeping your hair and nails done, smelling awesome, being kind and meek, and having healthy girlfriends will serve as your accountablity mechanism. Girlfriends will see what you cannot see (attributes and behavior traits that are red flags) because their insight comes from health and love rather than jealousy and envy. Be prepared to leave straggling men without a commitment bone in the past because wasting time with a straggler prolongs the unmarried season. Moreover, be a woman of prayer! Prayer will save lives and marriages, and there is no better time to begin practicing being a wife than the current day! Let us take a closer look at what marital preparation is like for the husband and the wife!

Marriage is for the grown and sexy! Both parties, husband and wife, must be fully-grown and mature adults. Women must not marry boys. Boys cannot handle the pressure of husbandry and therefore will not make good husbands. Men do not marry girls. Girls are not apt to hold the position or power of being a wife and carrying the responsibility of household, the cares of a husband, raising children, and imparting the anointing and glory into her atmosphere. Both immature subjects are not furnished with the authority or anointing to handle the pressures of becoming one and the lifestyle of marriage.

Husbands: Husband is defined in Greek as the "house-band," connecting and keeping together the whole family. A man when betrothed was esteemed from that time as a husband. Every male (married men included) are not "house-bands".

Did you ever hear the word "husband" explained? It literally means "the band of the house," the support of it, the person who keeps it together, as a band keeps together a sheaf of corn. There are many married men who are not husbands because they are not the band of the house. Truly, in many cases, the wife is the husband. Far often, it is she who, by her prudence, thrift, and economy, keeps the house together. This is disorderly in the realm of the spirit when the wife holds the family together. Thus, men (boys) feel a natural stripping of his manhood because he slipped out of his position due to silence, lack of input, being too laid back, or acting in pride. The married man, who by his dissolute habits strips his honour of all comfort, is not a husband. In a legal sense he is, but is not in the spiritual or as God designed a husband. For he is not a house-band. Instead of keeping things together, he scatters them among the pawnbrokers.

Now, here is a closer look at the word "wife," and it has a lesson too. It literally means weaver. The wife is the person who weaves. Before your great cotton and cloth factories arose, one of the principal employments in every house was the fabrication of clothing. Every family made its own. The wool was spun into thread by the girls who were therefore called spinsters. The thread was woven into cloth by their mother who accordingly was called the weaver, or the wife. Another remnant of this old truth you discover in the word is "heirloom," which is applied to any old piece of furniture that had come down to you from your ancestors. Though it may be a chair or bed, it shows that a loom was once a most important article in every house. The word "wife" means weaver; and, as Trench well remarks, "in the word itself is wrapped up a hint of earnest, indoor, stay-at-home occupations, as being fitted for her who bears this name."

Contrarily, wife in Hebrew and Greek is translated as woman. However, Proverbs 31:10-31 (KJV) as well as Proverbs 31:3 (KJV) gives a distinction in women and wife of virtue (woman of valor). A woman of valor or wife is defined below in accordance to scripture:

> *A worthy woman who can find? For her price is far above rubies. The heart of her husband trusteth in her, And he shall have no lack of gain. She doeth him good and not evil all the days of her life. She seeketh wool and flax, And worketh willingly with her hands. She is like the merchant-ships; She bringeth her bread from afar. She riseth also while it is yet night, And giveth food to her household, And their task to her maidens. She considereth a field, and buyeth it; With the fruit of her hands she planteth a vineyard. She girdeth her loins with strength, And maketh strong her arms. She perceiveth that her merchandise is profitable; Her lamp goeth not out by night. She layeth her hands to the distaff, And her hands hold the spindle. She stretcheth out her hand to the poor; Yea, she reacheth forth her hands to the needy. She is not afraid of the snow for her household; For all her household are clothed with scarlet. She maketh for herself carpets of tapestry; Her clothing is fine linen and purple. Her husband is known in the gates, When he sitteth among the elders of the land. She maketh linen garments and selleth them, And delivereth girdles unto the merchant. Strength and dignity are her clothing; And she laugheth at the time to come. She openeth her mouth with wisdom; And the law of kindness is on her tongue. She looketh well to the ways of her household, And eateth not the bread of idleness. Her children rise up, and call her blessed; Her husband also, and he praiseth her, saying: Many daughters have done worthily, But thou excellest them all. Grace is deceitful, and beauty is vain; But a woman that feareth Jehovah, she shall be praised. Give her of the fruit of her hands; And let her works praise her in the gates.*
>
> - PROVERBS 31:10-31 (ASV)

To summate Proverbs 31:10-31, here are traits of the standards and definition of a wife according to scripture, God's standard and definition!

- A wife of valor is priceless and an asset to her husband.
- Her husband can safely trust his heart with her.
- She is not fickle, inconsistent, impetuous, or unpredictable.
- Her character is consistent with consistent vision and values.
- Her will and motives towards her husband are good all the days of her life.
- She has his best interest at heart.
- She is a worker, a wife of valor that is a business woman and she willingly does so.
- She pulls inspiration from Jesus (Heaven) to feed her home spiritually and miraculously!
- She is concerned with her family's diet, health, food intake, and ensures there is food ready for them.
- She delegates tasks to those working for her and knows how to hire assistance. Moreover, she knows how to relinquish tasks and not control her environment, and does so with grace by instructing the maidens of their tasks so she is free to move in investments.
- She is an investor.
- She is firm in her salvation and persuasion of Jesus Christ.
- She is business savvy in the fact that her merchandise and investments are profitable to her and her home no matter the tasks or business dealing. Her "Light" will never go out! Her character is hidden in Christ and revealed in her godly manner.
- She has some domestic skills to assist her family and progress them forward.
- She is philanthropic, cares for those less fortunate, and has remedies to assist those that cross her path.

- She is not selfish.
- She is prepared for harsh weather, and her family lives in preparedness because of her forethought.
- She clothes herself with holiness, dignity, and honor.
- She does not neglect her own appearance and dresses queenly.
- She speaks with wisdom and love. Kindness keeps the gate of her mouth.
- Her husband is honored in the land, and known in the courts of heaven due to her prayer life.
- She is a lioness with an eagle eye.
- She watches the atmosphere of her home.
- She is the eyes when spirits are threatening the entrance of her home.
- Nothing enters in her home past her being the wiser.
- Her family testifies to being happy, fortunate, and blessed having her as wife and mother.
- The family acknowledges they advance in the kingdom of God and their spheres of influence.
- She is a woman (wife of valor) that fears the Lord above beauty and riches.
- The heavens declare the works she's done produces her heavenly reward, and her own works praise her at the gates!

On the other hand, being a basic woman (women run of the mill) has her traits as well…. *"Give not thy strength unto women, Nor thy ways to that which destroyeth kings." -Proverbs 31:3 (ASV)*. Consequently, King Lemuel's mother warns him not to entertain such a woman.

King Lemuel's mother, Queen, definitely made a distinction between women who are plenteous and easy to obtain in any given whim, while generally not potential virtuous woman (wife of valor) material. That word women in Hebrew is translated as "ishshah" which means harlot, adulteress, frail, weak, desperately sick soul, an incurable soul (TouchBible App., Strongs Version). And, in addition to the Queen warning her son about these particular types of women, she adds, *"Nor your ways to that which continuously destroys kings."* This means that having unrighteous ways and whoremongering or being an adulterer are ways that destroys the lives of kings. Women with those traits destroy the king in men and cause them not to see or acknowledge the queen (lady in waiting) in a woman.

Trapping a man with sex to draw him emotionally does not make you a wife. Having sex with a man does not prove to him that you are ready for lasting commitment. In reality, sex is a spiritual/soulical/bodily bonding agent, and it will concrete a man's unwillingness to never commit to you. Men, rather men that are husband material, desire the conquest of a committed woman, not a woman that is a play thing. That woman will remain just that... a woman he can call to get his release with. Not a woman that commands wifehood respect. I once asked my daddy as a teenager, "What made you want to marry momma?" His real and earnest response was, "I knew that I wanted to make your mom my wife when I saw that she was not to be played with, that I cannot just come over her house and stay, and that I had to [and she commanded] respect." Sex is important to both men and women; however, creating an atmosphere of respect, honor, patience, and commitment is twice as important when building a covenant.

# II

## Thou Shalt Know The Origination Of Marriage

*And God said, Let us make man in your image, after your likeness: and let them have dominion over the fish of the sea, and over the fowl of the air, and over the cattle, and over all the earth, and over every creeping thing that creepeth upon the earth. So God created man in his own image, in the image of God created he him; male and female created he them. And God blessed them, and God said unto them, Be fruitful, and multiply, and replenish the earth, and subdue it: and have dominion over the fish of the sea, and over the fowl of the air, and over every living thing that moveth upon the earth.*

- **Genesis 1:26 (KJV)**

GOD the Father is the progenitor of marriage. Your lineage, legacy, and longevity of marriage flows from His Person. When God originated marriage, He had your future in mind! It is amazing that when a mother is carrying her daughter, she carries her potential granddaughter! The very ovaries that rest in the mother's womb have already been created and are the very same ovaries that hold her future grandchildren! God had you all in mind in the like manner!

God created marriage to speak to generations of productivity, multiplication, and lineage extension for creating an "everlasting kingdom of sons of God." These generations will take over and dominate situations, scenarios, and dominate kingdoms and obstacles that stand in the way

8

of the plan of God. It is funny how Satan's main attack against your marriages is to thwart the original intent from the command of God, which was to: *"Be fruitful, and multiply, and replenish the earth, and subdue it: and have dominion over the fish of the sea, and over the fowl of the air, and over every living thing that moveth upon the earth."* Genesis 1:26 (KJV). The devil loves to stop fruitfulness (productivity) by less-than-desired credit scores, negative bank accounts, and working more than enjoying life with your spouse. Unfortunately, you only end up with empty pockets, a few bills paid, foreclosures, evictions, and repossessions. Not creating businesses or systems of wealth to break the power of poverty prevailing in the home causes arguments and aggression.

The Hebrew meaning for multiplication is *rabah*, meaning to be or become much, many or great, meaning increase, expand, be great, multiply, increase, greatly increase, enlarge, make great, make much to do, do much, abundantly; greatly, often, make large, increase, grow and be great, make numerous, and become many. Your identity in Christ is to be great, and do big things— lots of big, abundant things. Moreover, when we do these big, great things in abundance, we multiply the works. The enemy fights marriages inside of identity in Christ Jesus by hindering your own personal growth and the two becoming one. The devil hinders your power to multiply and be great. He loves to keep you in small spaces, never growing together, never discovering or emerging and expanding into your destiny. He throws distractions of brokenness, poverty, lust, drugs, alcohol abuse, depression, and mental illness to keep you locked out of your true potential in God, which was commanded to you to produce continual prosperity, peace, and power in your lives and lineages. With that being said, *"replenish the earth."* This is where Satan shows contempt towards humankind by kidnapping and holding

9

lineages for ransom from conception! Satan hates when we conceive sons of God! Your lineage in the earth is a literal threat to the kingdom of darkness! Satan loves infertility, miscarriages, abortions, post partum depression, rejection, abandonment, sex outside of the confines of marriage (homosexual sex and adultery sex), producing children outside of marriage, and rebellion.

Often times you think, "it is better to marry than burn;" but you use this scripture to jutify having sex outside of marriage and then rush to get married. Marriage does not cure the soulical issue of lust and perversion and neither does it kill lust! If you do not heal from molestation, rape, pornography, and premarital sex, you will freely give away jurisdiction to the devil to sow seeds of discord and deception into the marriage. Once it crops up, you won't be prepared for the yield of this fruit in marriage. The produce of these grounds can be adultery in the marriage, pornography in the marriage, spouse's hurt and offended by the introduction of pornography in the marriage, children who battle with their sexuality, and children who fall into demonic generational curses of lust and perversion.

## *Marriage is Delight*

*And the Lord God formed man of the dust of the ground, and breathed into his nostrils the breath of life; and man became a living soul. And the Lord God planted a garden eastward in Eden; and there he put the man whom he had formed. And out of the ground made the Lord God to grow every tree that is pleasant to the sight, and good for food; the tree of life also in the midst of the garden, and the tree of knowledge of good and evil. And a river went out of Eden to water the garden; and from thence it was parted, and became into your heads. The name of the first is Pison: that is it which compasseth the whole land of Havilah, where there is gold; And the gold of that land is good: there is bdellium and the onyx stone. And the name of the second river is Gihon: the same is it that compasseth the whole land of Ethiopia. And the name of the third river is Hiddekel: that is it, which goeth toward the east of Assyria. And the fourth river is Euphrates. And the Lord God took the man, and put him into the Garden of Eden to dress it and to keep it. And the Lord God commanded the man, saying, Of every tree of the garden thou mayest freely eat: But of the tree of the knowledge of good and evil, thou shalt not eat of it: for in the day that thou eatest thereof thou shalt surely die. And the Lord God said, It is not good that the man should be alone; I will make him an help meet for him. And out of the ground the Lord God formed every beast of the field, and every fowl of the air; and brought them unto Adam to see what he would call them: and whatsoever Adam called every living creature, that was the name thereof. And Adam gave names to all cattle, and to the fowl of the air, and to every beast of the field; but for Adam there was not found an help meet for him. And the Lord God caused a deep sleep to fall upon Adam, and he slept: and he took one of his ribs, and closed up the flesh instead thereof; And the rib, which the Lord God had taken from man, made he a woman, and brought her unto the man. And Adam said, This is now bone of my bones, and flesh of my flesh: she shall be called Woman, because she was taken out of Man. Therefore shall a man leave his father and his mother, and shall cleave unto his wife: and they shall be one flesh. And they were both naked, the man and his wife, and were not ashamed.*

                                        - GENESIS 2:7-25

As you closely pay attention to the aforementioned scripture, you find that Adam was not created in Eden. Before Adam was created, there was no rain (as of yet) and no one to tend to the earth and encourage earth to replicate seeds through tilling the ground. God formed man out of the dust of the ground, as He has created all of the Earth. Without there being reference to Adam and God's relationship, there is a literal metaphor of their relationship. After Adam was created, God was designing and preparing Adam for Eden (The Place of Delight). God was already in touch with Adam's need. Though Adam was building a relationship with His Father, God was creating a geographical and situational place of delight and fulfillment for Adam!

*Trust in the Lord, and do good; so shalt thou dwell in the land, and verily thou shalt be fed. Delight thyself also in the Lord; and he SHALT give thee the desires of thine heart. Commit thy way unto the Lord; trust also in him; and he SHALT bring it to pass. And he SHALT bring forth thy righteousness as the light, and thy judgment as the noonday.*

                                        - PSALMS 37:4-9

As you delight yourselves in God, your Father, He knits together your futures. Your major issue is trying to perfect His perfect timing. Marriage happens properly when you trust in God. Trusting God speaks to having a relationship with Him! Adam's relationship with God moves Him to place Adam in a land of Delight (Eden). Inside of Eden, Adam again finds himself, caring for the garden, the plants, and animals. Moreover, Adam is caring for the maintenance of God's heart which is caring for the grounds of Eden. This in turn causes God to look upon Adam and see his need, and for the first time God says, "It is not good." Throughout the history or generations of the Earth, everything God had done and created was, "Good." When God sees that Adam does not have a helpmeet, like all of the other animals, He sees the loneliness in Adam. Although Adam had a Father who indeed loved him, was there for him and held a good relationship with him, Adam did not have anyone suitable for him. God recognized Adam's need. God does not change. He recognizes your need.

The most powerful thing about God recognizing Adam's need is the humble sincerity of God to say, "although I Am everything, I have the ability to provide and do everything. However, there is one thing I Am not to my son, a helpmeet." This does not diminish God in relationship. It makes Him even more powerful! This fact gave room for God to create something new! God did something He has never done in all creation of Earth! Instead of forming another human woman out of the Earth, He puts Adam to sleep (some would say the idea of medical science Anesthesia comes from this), opens his side, takes rib and flesh, closes him up, and makes a woman. After God created Woman (Eve), He presents her to Adam! Adam recognizes that she was pulled out of him and that these two are one in the eyes of God. Marriage was a unique institution that God created!

The theory of two human beings sharing one frame and wholeness (of person) and completion is awesome! Moreover, this all happened in Eden. The original design of marriage was oneness and delight! In the mind of God concerning marriage is a placement of purity, unification, holiness, relationship, companionship, monogamy, and love! Marriage was created in the Garden of Eden, which means in the placement of delight. The family unit however was created in the world! Adam and Eve were evicted out of the Garden of Eden due to the fall. The heavy burdened with curses, pressures of life, and raising children began.

# III

## THIS IS WHAT MARRIAGE LOOKS LIKE
### (REALITY VS. MEDIA)

Marriage in everyday life is not to be confused with daydreams, movies, television, and social media. Television solves marriage woes in thirty minutes or in a two part series. However, in reality, the issues within the marriage, i.e. foundation underpinnings, spouse, and spouse's upbringing will not be solved in a matter of minutes or moments. Hard issues may take months, may take years, may take revisiting issues and tabling issues, may take conflict and resolution, and may take investing in marriage through counseling, retreats, or marriage groups in church. We idolize and place the thought of the image (what we think marriage should be) of marriage above the reality of marriage (what you and your spouse really are.) Image worship is the sin of idolatry. Idolatry in the Greek is *eidlon* and is defined as "image" or "fantasy".

Eidlon originally meant "image" or "fantasy." By the time of the Septuagint, the term was used for images of gods. "Idolatry" is literally "image worship." To grasp the character of image worship in biblical literature, one must first realize that the Bible describes the worship of all "strange gods" as idolatry or the worship of "wood and stone." In addition, one must distinguish the biblical polemics against these gods from the opposition to the use of certain images in the service of Yahweh. At times the use of these images were equated with the service of other gods. *(https://www.jewishvirtuallibrary.org/idolatry)*

When you glamorize what you think your marriage, spouse, or the idea of marriage should be, you are in the sin of idolatry. You mark your spouse and marriage for destruction when it is compared and held up to a false image (fantasy). You attempt to meet that mark instead of the mark of your high callings together in Christ Jesus! Truth being, marriage is designed to make you holy and come into the image of Christ. Any other image is an idol. Idols are always up for destruction and minimization by a jealous God.

*And the Philistines took the ark of God, and brought it from Ebenezer unto Ashdod. When the Philistines took the ark of God, they brought it into the house of Dagon, and set it by Dagon. And when they of Ashdod arose early on the morrow, behold, Dagon was fallen upon his face to the earth before the ark of the Lord. And they took Dagon, and set him in his place again. And when they arose early on the morrow morning, behold, Dagon was fallen upon his face to the ground before the ark of the Lord; and the head of Dagon and both the palms of his hands were cut off upon the threshold; only the stump of Dagon was left to him. Therefore neither the priests of Dagon, nor any that come into Dagon's house, tread on the threshold of Dagon in Ashdod unto this day. But the hand of the Lord was heavy upon them of Ashdod, and he destroyed them, and smote them with emerods, even Ashdod and the coasts thereof. And when the men of Ashdod saw that it was so, they said, The ark of the God of Israel shall not abide with you: for his hand is sore upon you, and upon Dagon your god. They sent therefore and gathered all the lords of the Philistines unto them, and said, What shall we do with the ark of the God of Israel? And they answered, Let the ark of the God of Israel be carried about unto Gath. And they carried the ark of the God of Israel about thither. And it was so, that, after they had carried it about, the hand of the Lord was against the city with a very great destruction: and he smote the men of the city, both small and great, and they had emerods in their secret parts. Therefore they sent the ark of God to Ekron. And it came to pass, as the ark of God came to Ekron, that the Ekronites cried out, saying, They have brought about the ark of the God of Israel to us, to slay us and our people. So they sent and gathered together all the lords of the Philistines, and said, Send away the ark of the God of Israel, and let it go again to his own place, that it slay you not, and your people: for there was a deadly destruction throughout all the city; the hand of God was very heavy there. And the men that died not were smitten with the emerods: and the cry of the city went up to heaven.*

— 1 Samuel 5:1-12

You are designed to love God, and serve Him only; and put no other "gods" before Him. However, when you idolize and over-desire marriage, idolize your spouse, or idolize the image of what you think marriage should look like, there will come destruction and a leveling of the playing field for the idol to submit to Christ. God's justice is fair and righteous in delivering and healing the parts of you that will idolize your spouse or the institution of marriage (an institution God created).

Moreover, when we allow the media, which means *middle ground* in Latin, to rule your gates or senses (eyes, ears, nose, mouth), it has free course to rule and operate depraved within your hearts, minds, will, and emotions. Thinking and comparison with someone else's middle ground through what is seemingly happy on social media or a happy couple on television is literally a battleground where the daydreamer is loosing arguments, mental anguish, and stress over the personal process to deliverance. Failure in marriage does not occur until both spouses decide to stop fighting and trying to be something they are not. Each day when a spouse wakes up and there is an argument, a disagreement, a money battle, or a lack of sex battle— is a day that the marriage is winning!

Do not bring comparison or false realities into marriage. Every marriage is unique. The process God employs to deliverance is unique and also depends on several unique factors: how submitted is each partner to the process? Are both partners ready to let go of learned harmful ideologies, habits, upbringing behaviors, unhealthy communication styles, demonic methodologies, and individualism? Moreover, ask the Lord to redeem the imagery of marriage. Understanding that you are made "in Their (Father, Son, Holy Spirit) image and after Their Likeness," and as a result, you cannot form a marriage or lifestyle in the image of the world!

> *And do not be conformed to this world, but be transformed by the renewing of your mind, so that you may prove what the will of God is, that which is good and acceptable and perfect. Therefore I urge you, brethren, by the mercies of God, to present your bodies a living and holy sacrifice, acceptable to God, which is your spiritual service of worship.*
>
> - ROMANS 12:2

Most images that come through media i.e., social media, news, sitcoms, and movies are a secular world-view of how fallen nature defines marriage. Media and secular image has not been confounded or transformed into the image of Christ. Therefore, the only thing a secular image can do for a marriage is cause the spirit of death, which is divorce and separation. The worst thing you can do is measure your marriages against sitcoms. Sitcoms will ruin entire lives, lineages, and legacies. False images destroy lives and marriages! Renew your mind today! Ask the Holy Spirit to deal with strongholds (high places of your mindset that have not been transformed to Christ Jesus.

Renewing your mind and coming into the image of God and Christlikeness in marriage will teach you how to:
- Minister to your spouse's deepest need and desires.
- Love them properly through the lenses of scripture which will fill voids and incompetencies in their life.
- Compromise with them.
- Converse effectively with them.
- Teach you how to make love to them.

In addition, having the image of Christ formed in you shows you how to properly handle life's issues in marriage healthily and overcome them. It also directs you in real life affairs and takes off the stigma of expectations of what a good marriage looks like. Your personal marriages are perfect with their flaws, failures, and successes. Life and longevity of marriage depends on becoming the image of Christ. BEING the image and likeness of Jesus Christ is paramount! When we reflect the image and likeness of Christ, we behave, think, speak, act, and perform day-to-day tasks. The image and likeness of Christ looks like the following:

- Patience with your spouse and children
- Loving unconditionally when you do not always feel like it
- Hope when all things feel as though it is failing and there is not a reason to continue with marriage
- Faith to move mountains when everything is standing in the way (illness, jobs, school, money, sex life, bad communication, arguments and differences of opinion)

Marriage is designed to make you holy. Marriage will challenge the depths of your Christlikeness and cause you to draw closer to the image of God. As you have to continuously look at His image to see where you are lacking discipline, spiritual awareness, behavior conflict, and speech deficits in your character, you will be made conformable to His image. The more you challenge and see your deficits, the more humble you become as your need arises for Christ. The more hungry and thirsty you are for Christ, the more He imbues you with His character (fruit of the Spirit), image, likeness, and power. Hence, being more filled with Christ's image and likeness, you can have patience when you want to curse, fight, exact revenge (get justice for wrongdoings), go tit-for-tat (bicker back and forth without resolve), have an attitude, be mean and selfish, and keep record of wrongs. Marriage is a divine mirror that will reveal how much more you need Jesus and His person to manifest on the inside of you! His character glorified in you will knock out every ungodly lesson, communication, nonverbal teaching, verbal teaching, and traumatic instance that you have received from childhood, and grow you into a godly, mature, and prepared people to inspire good works to the world!

# IV

## THOU SHALT KEEP YOUR VOWS

*When thou shalt vow a vow unto the LORD thy God, thou shalt not slack to pay it: for the LORD thy God will surely require it of thee; and it would be sin in thee.*
**- DEUTERONOMY 23:21**

Y ou must always remember that the keywords in getting married are "vows." You get married and undertake vows to the love of your life, and pledge your undying love and affections to this one person. However, it is much deeper than pledging vows to the love of a lifetime. It is pledging vows to a Holy God! God is the originator of covenant and becomes an instant part of your covenant. Meaning, the vows we undertake are not just to the proposed spouse, but it automatically involves God into the equation. You are automatically undertaking your vows to God! Marriage is bigger than just the initial wedding day and saying cute things because you feel chemistry and butterflies at the sight of the object of your affections. The words you speak, repeat, and agree to (promise and spiritual contractually agree to), hold spiritual gravity and authority to govern your character, integrity, and futures!

### The Importance of Cutting Covenant

The word covenant in the Hebrew is *berîyth*, which means to "cut," or "cutting." When marriage covenant and vows are complete, there is a cutting, release, and more cutting as a marriage institution is designed to make you holy. However, there is another occurrence at work! Some suggest that parties of the covenant are thereby saying in essence, "May I be torn apart like these animals if I fail to uphold my part of this covenant." This is illustrated in Genesis 15, as God alone passes between the slaughtered animals while Abraham sleeps, again emphasizing the unilateral nature of this covenant, as well as the ultimate level of commitment involved— God putting his very life on the line as a guarantee. Hence, everything in scripture revolves around the issue of covenant, including Old Testament and New Testament, which are also old covenant contract and new covenant contract between you, Christ Jesus, Heaven, Earth, and Hell. Moreover, Christ puts His life on the line for this covenant and guarantees your covenant through His bloodshed.

Marriage vows and covenants are just as equally important as long as there is blood pumping through the veins of living spouses under holy circumstances. At the point of consummation, blood is shed by the penetrating of your wife's hymen.

> For the life of the flesh is in the blood: and I have given it to you upon the altar to make an atonement for your souls: for it is the blood that maketh an atonement for the soul.
>
> - LEVITICUS 17:11

Your covenant is still yet valid and speaks in a multidimensional fashion [Earth, Heaven, and Hell]. With this being said, there are three crucial components of divine covenant that have been outlined above: unilateral establishment, relational bond, and ultimate commitment. Each of these aspects is brought out in covenant. Palmer Robertson's definition of covenant is *"a bond in blood sovereignly administered."* As a result, you find the nature of God's covenant. "God's covenants contain two especially important components: terms and duration. Although people may reach covenants or other agreements through their own devices, God's covenants with people are usually unilateral. God alone determines the terms and conditions; and people choose whether to accept them." However, everyone who freely accepts their vows and covenants, while also performing and keeping them, reaps the rewards in Genesis 15 as a descendant of Abraham in receiving land, descendants, and blessings! Moreover, there are consequences for dishonoring, breaking, disannulling, and disobeying God in covenant.

## Vows Up Close

Let's take a closer look at your traditional Christian vows, by Thomas Crammer, Archbishop of Canterbury:

*I, _____, take thee _____, to be my wedded husband/wife, to have and to hold from this day forward, for better for worse, for richer or for poorer, in sickness and in health, to love and to cherish, 'til death do you part, according to God's ordinance; and thereto I pledge thee my troth.*

*Officiant: Will you, _____; have _____ to be your husband/wife? Will you love him/her, comfort and keep him/her, and forsaking all others remain true to him/her as long as you both SHALT live?"*
*Wedded couple (together or individually): I Do.*

*Officiant: _____ do you take _____ to be your husband/wife? Do you promise to love, honor, cherish and protect him/her, forsaking all others and holding only to him/her forevermore?*

*Groom/Bride: I do.*

(Rings Exchange)

*With this ring I thee wed, and all my worldly goods I thee endow. In sickness and in health, in poverty or in wealth, 'til death do you part.*

As we observe in the aforementioned vows, you observe the following terms: richer or poorer, sickness and in health, good times and bad times, forsaking all others (being faithful) and duration (death do you part). You also see the illusion of God and relationship between Him and yourself. This is the foundation of most marriage covenants. As God cuts covenant with you, He is also symbolizing that He– by His power will upkeep these vows until, *"death do you part;"* Otherwise, may He and We be split like those animals that were cut in half! This is why divorce hurts so badly. You are in essence cutting (ripping away) the spouse and God (covenant grantor) apart from the contract of God who has also cut covenant with you. There is a tearing away spiritually and naturally (emotions, heartbreak, mental awareness (illness) and will (survival/ thriving mechanism). All of these areas shut off or weakens. However, take a closer look at Biblical Judaism marital covenant (vows) customs.

### Biblical Judaism Marriage Customs

In Biblical times, it was unusual to marry someone foreign with different belief systems because they caused the sons/daughters to be introduced to strange gods. To prevent such unions, the fathers negotiated a match for their children. Oftentimes, they married in their youth. Ages 13-15 was considered adulthood in biblical times. In those days a father was more concerned about the marriage of his sons than about the marriage of his daughters. There was no expense involved in marrying off a daughter. The father received a dowry for his daughter. On the other hand, he had to give a dowry to the prospective father-in-law of his son when marrying him off. It is shown here how marriage reflects the heart of God and salvation and how Jesus Christ gave his life [the Father's most expensive dowry] for the Church [His Bride].

The price paid by the Father of the Groom was called a mohar and mattan. "Mattan" was the Hebrew word for the gifts given by the groom to the bride in addition to the mohar. The "mohar" was not always paid in cash. Sometimes it was paid in kindness or in service. This is traditionally known as the Ketubah Marriage Contract. The biblical example of this transaction can be found in Genesis 29 and 34 [Jacob and Rebekah/Leah and Dinah]. This is the contract that is signed giving honor, respect, gifts, money, and service to the family and wife in the transaction of marriage. Nowadays, this is the father consenting to give away his daughter free of cost. Understanding this, the mohar was originally the purchase price of the bride, and it is therefore understandable why it was paid by the father of the groom to the father of the bride.

In ancient days, marriage was not an agreement between two individuals (as now brides are given away free of cost), but between two families (replacing one family member with a pricey cost that has the ability to bring worth and prosperity to the family). The newlyweds did not usually find a home for themselves, but lived in the father's house of the groom (Naomi and Ruth- Ruth Chapter One). The father-of-the-groom gained a working occupant as well as the older couple taught the younger couple customs of marriage. The family of the groom gained while the family of the bride lost a valuable member who helped with all household tasks. It was reasonable that the father of the groom should pay the father of the bride the equivalent of her value as a useful member of the family. However, over time the mohar lost its original meaning as a purchase price paid to the father for his daughter and assumed the significance of a gift to the near relatives of the bride.

In early biblical times, it was customary for a good father to give the whole of the mohar or at least a large part of it to his daughter. A father who appropriated the whole mohar for himself was considered unkind and unjust. The portion of the mohar that the bride received from her father and the mattan, which the groom presented to her, was not the only possession she brought to matrimony. A rich father sometimes gave his daughter a field or other land property as well as female slaves. In contrast, to current day, there is no promise or price given to the father in respect to ensure good behavior and promise of longevity of marriage. Because marriage is freely given now, it is mishandled and treated unfairly. In retrospect, in Biblical era marriage consisted of two ceremonies that were celebrated at two separate times with an interval between the times of celebration. First came the betrothal [eryouin] and later, the wedding [nissuin]. Though the woman still remained in her fathers house, the betrothal meant she was legally married. She could not belong to another man unless she was divorced from her betrothed. The wedding only meant that the betrothed woman accompanied by a colorful procession was brought from her father's house to the house of her groom; and the legal tie with him was consummated. Marriage, as with any type of purchase, consisted of two acts. First, the price was paid and an agreement was reached on the conditions of sale. This is where we find that Jesus buys back his bride from sin, death, and judgment [Passion of Christ and Calvary] through the purchase of his blood covenant and taking on His Name as the highest name of all; and everything the bride suffers breaks in her husband's (Jesus') name. Sometime later, the husband took possession of the wife. This is Jesus going away to prepare a place for you where He is also.

In marriage, the mohar was paid and a detailed agreement reached between the families of the bride and groom. The betrothal was then followed by the wedding and the bride being brought into the home of the groom who took actual possession of her. In those days, the betrothal (current day engagement) was the more important of these two events and maintained its importance as long as the marriage was actually based upon a purchase. But as women were assumed more important as individuals and marriage ceased to be a purchase (attaining moral significance), the actual wedding became more important than the betrothal. Moreover, the wedding comes free of cost to the family of the groom and the responsibility fell onto the family of the bride (traditional wedding setting). Today, the highest cost (traditionally) is the potential groom asking the potential bride's father for her hand in marriage and receiving a rejection from the bride's father. However, if the couple still desired marriage, they could possibly elope! When this switching and modernization of marriage occurred (lessening the importance of engagement and emphasis on wedding and family of the bride), Christiandom cheapened the biblical significance, prize, price, possession, and meaning. Nonetheless, if we bring into the biblical account of being betrothed and the significance of marriage, we will see clearly the nature of marriage through a heavenly perspective. Marriage is designed to make you holy. It removes the stench of earthly greed, sin nature, lust, and perversion and introduces you to a God who loves you and is concerned so much about you that He set up a worthy cost, payed it, and redeemed you. Marriage, in its purest form teaches you redemption power. Selah.

This is why God cuts covenant with you and makes it difficult for Him and you to break so you may learn the depths of redemption and the truth that we are all worthy no matter what you say, do, or think; and that there is no going backwards and ripping covenant (vows) because the price has already been paid. Marriage teaches you to hone a love that covers a multitude of sins. In addition, we see the terms, conditions, and duration within this marital covenant. Marriage covenant was a transactional relationship with a transformational promise for the duration of life as God is the grantor, and those of you (they in Biblical era) are the partakers of this marriage covenant. And, in keeping your covenant vows before God, you are honoring the Godhead, yourselves, your legacy, and your lineage. Moreover, you are creating an everlasting covenant for generational wealth, health, and blessings to beget your sons and daughters, both natural and spiritual.

# V

## THOU SHALT BECOME ONE

*Therefore shall a man leave his father and his mother, and shall cleave unto his wife: and they shall be one flesh.*
**- GENESIS 2:24**

Oftentimes when young and old read this scripture, we automatically attribute oneness to sex. However, this scripture and others alike that read, *"two shall become one flesh"* is not to be limited to a sex life when it means the total summation of the entire marriage life. *"Become one flesh,"* primarily means becoming one is a process. This process is leaving both backgrounds you have previously been accustomed to, such as: communication styles, expectations, triggers, thoughts, and behaviors from your childhood or previous unmarried lifestyle—to becoming one in communication style, thought process, behavior, triggers, expectations, boundaries, and family. Becoming one most of the time brings about disagreements and arguments. Arguments are not just for argument sake! Arguing happens to bring solutions and draw the focus, intentionality, and marriage closer in unity. Arguments are healthy when they are solution driven. Becoming one or the process of becoming one is friction driven. You will not just wake up, marry, and become one because of sex. Oneness or unity takes time, and the time for becoming one does not happen instantly or during the "honeymoon phase" of the marriage. Because marriage is an ongoing way of life, becoming one is an ongoing process. Oneness is unity. Unity is God produced. The devil or the devilish disrupts unity by bringing discord and disunity. There are specific responsibilities for believers in unity. Your biblical responsibility for oneness within marriage includes:

- Being united of one mind and thought
- Agreeing so there will be no divisions among you
- Becoming mature in Christ and attaining the full measure of Christ
- Having patience with your spouse and forgiving if you have any issues with them as Christ Jesus forgave you for your trespasses
- Putting on love which will unify you in forgiveness
- Being like-minded, sympathetic, humble and compassionate
- Being a peacemaker
- Both spouses placing Jesus as teacher and savior to lead the way of unity as He compels unity within the Body of Christ and is the Head of you all
- Withstanding, having the hand of God upon both spouses to accomplish that which He has commanded you
- Being dead to sin nature and alive through resurrection life
- Putting away the gratification of the flesh
- Demonstrating grace and mercy
- Recognizing and appreciating your differences but embracing your sameness
- You being male and female but one in Christ
- Forbidding any walls of hostility to grow within marriage
- Living in unity
- Demonstrating the love of God within the marriage

As we can see, oneness is a responsibility within marriage and the body of Christ at large. You are both held responsible for bringing about disunity within your marriages. Although arguments may start in the mind or heart of one spouse, it really does take both spouses to birth out disunity and separation of the unit. When two people get married, the covenant and soul of marriage naturally drives the two individuals together. Marriage strips off individuality and causes a special bond to be formed. This bond or yoking together causes both persons in the marriage to walk together with the same stride, finish each other's sentences, and desire the same things in life. This is the beauty of marriage; however, the grinding away of individual thoughts, selfishness, and prideful self-seeking intentions do not happen overnight. In fact, most couples fight constantly about areas in life that they want to hold on to. These are the perceived positions of power in the relationship such as controlling interests where one person's interest is met and the other person's interest is overlooked, when one person's belief is levied over another's, or when the other has the position to nitpick, simply being argumentative, and choosing to disagree.

All of these stimulate the position of separation. This demonic force is so scary because it infiltrates the marriage in the onset as statements that open the doors for such. For example, you are two different people and you are supposed to disagree. Now understand in truth, marriage is composed of two people coming together from two different backgrounds and behavior patterns, so disagreements do happen; but the extreme positions of disagreement and constant disagreement releases disunity and separation. It breaks down marriages both young and old. Older marriages open this door by statements like, "I'm too old to change," or "we are always on different pathways."

The power of agreement is the only power that heals disunity:

Can two walk together, except they be agreed?
- AMOS 3:3

Marriage is the journey of two people walking together in syncopation. Learning to be in sync with someone is an art. It requires having the same timing, thoughts, and beliefs. Your marriage should reside in this place. To be agreeable, in agreement, or agreed means that both spouses have had conversation about the most important things in life and found common mind. Common mind in relationships are entirely necessary. Without common mind, the space of the relationship becomes rocky and unstable, creating insecurity in both spouses. Oneness is coming together consistently in total compatibility and commonality. The goal in every marriage is oneness.

*Again I say unto you, That if two of you shall agree on earth as touching anything that they shall ask, it shall be done for them of my Father which is in heaven.*

- MATTHEW 18:19

This is the power of agreement. All of Heaven, its creation, and God stands with those that walk in the spirit of agreement. When a couple wants to see miracles, they merge their hearts, and faith together in agreement to see it done. Couples that are in constant strife will never see the power of God manifest. Favor and blessing are reserved for those that operate with the spirit of agreement. Oneness irons out the wrinkles of life. Oneness opens the doors of Heaven and releases the overflow. Strife and disunity creates obstacles, craters, stumbling, and a constant feeling of failure in the marriage. On the other hand, when both spouses choose to submit to one another, a victorious you or a winning spirit is endowed upon them. The traps that other marriages fall into are avoided. The power of prayer awakens in the marriage and truly anything that the couple chooses to pray for happens. This is the truth behind good marriages. They have learned the secret of becoming one with one another.

# VI

## Thou Shalt Submit

*Submitting yourselves one to another in the fear of God. Wives, submit yourselves unto your own husbands, as unto the Lord. For the husband is the head of the wife, even as Christ is the head of the church: and he is the saviour of the body. Therefore as the church is subject unto Christ, so let the wives be to their own husbands in everything. Husbands, love your wives, even as Christ also loved the church, and gave himself for it; That he might sanctify and cleanse it with the washing of water by the word, That he might present it to himself a glorious church, not having spot, or wrinkle, or any such thing; but that it should be holy and without blemish. So ought men to love their wives as their own bodies. He that loveth his wife loveth himself. For no man ever yet hated his own flesh; but nourisheth and cherisheth it, even as the Lord the church: For we are members of his body, of his flesh, and of his bones. For this cause shall a man leave his father and mother, and shall be joined unto his wife, and they two shall be one flesh. This is a great mystery: but I speak concerning Christ and the church. Nevertheless let every one of you in particular so love his wife even as himself; and the wife see that she reverence her husband.*

**- Ephesians 5:21-33**

Oftentimes in church, religious folks will create malignant scriptural references that only require wives to submit to unsubmitted husbands. This creates a dangerous environment in the household where a prideful husband refuses to submit to anyone, including God, and inflicts the house with abuse. Submission to one another is omitted through religious, pious, and chauvinistic saints. Women are either confused about the implementation of submission or totally rebel against submission. Throughout scripture, when everyone is in submission to authority, it causes God, the ultimate authority to respond in strength. When you lack submission, you lack order. When you lack order, you lack a supernatural environment in the home that produces favor, healing, and blessings.

A lack of submission to authority is called, "willful rebellion." Rebellion in scripture is judged as witchcraft.

> *For rebellion is as the sin of witchcraft, and stubbornness is as iniquity and idolatry. Because thou hast rejected the word of the Lord, he hath also rejected thee from being king.*
>
> - 1 SAMUEL 15:23

Witchcraft is synonymous with divination, which literally means a divine decision to turn away from God and His laws. Submission to God and His laws keeps you holy and away from witchcraft and familiar spirits (demons and sin nature) where you receive information and strategy to lead your own life absent of the Father. Additionally, stubbornness is as iniquity and idolatry, which means that being stubborn in marriage and attempting to hang onto a position very rigidly is "image-worship or divine honour paid to any created object." This is when self-image or what you think and how you feel is elevated above God's truth.

On the other hand, rebellion coupled with willfully walking in familiar spirits to get information and leading your life separate from God is also knowing the right thing to do and deliberately choosing your own path and position. See why rebellion and witchcraft are synonymous? You are living your life knowing the right way to go but deliberately choosing the wrong way to go. One may ask, "Well I do not know scripture well, now what?" Here's what Jesus said:

> *When the Spirit of truth comes, he will guide you into all truth. He will not speak on his own but will tell you what he has heard. He will tell you about the future. He will bring me glory by telling you whatever he receives from me. All that belongs to the Father is mine; this is why I said, 'The Spirit will tell you whatever he receives from me.*
>
> - JOHN 16:13-15

Holy Spirit is the part of the Triune Godhead and of the Spirit of God sent by Jesus to lead you into all truth.

Holy Spirit will unction in you the right way to go, how to lead your life, give you revelation on how to maneuver circumstances in your life, and how to posture your heart and mind in relationships and marriage. In contrast, when you ignore the Holy Spirit's impression and go your own way, you grieve Holy Spirit by falling out of agreement and partnering with witchcraft and idolatry [your ways of thinking and doing above Holy Spirit's ways].

> *Do not let unwholesome [foul, profane, worthless, vulgar] words ever come out of your mouth, but only such speech as is good for building up others, according to the need and the occasion, so that it will be a blessing to those who hear [you speak]. And do not grieve the Holy Spirit of God [but seek to please Him], by whom you were sealed and marked [branded as God's own] for the day of redemption [the final deliverance from the consequences of sin]. Let all bitterness and wrath and anger and clamor [perpetual animosity, resentment, strife, fault-finding] and slander be put away from you, along with every kind of malice [all spitefulness, verbal abuse, malevolence]. Be kind and helpful to one another, tender-hearted [compassionate, understanding], forgiving one another [readily and freely], just as God in Christ also forgave you.*
>
> - EPHESIANS 4:29-32 (AMP)

The following are grievous behaviors that exhibit a lack of submission and willful rebellion to the unction of the Holy Spirit: bitterness, resentment, strife, fault-finding, slander, malice, spitefulness, verbal abuse, malevolence, and using foul and vulgar words. Listen up! You need Holy Spirit to make your marriage work and teach you how to submit in marriage according to REAL scriptural implications.

### Truth of Submission

Firstly, in order to submit you must enlist the Holy Spirit for revelation of submission within your OWN marriage. What works spiritually and naturally in one marriage may not work in another. You may need Holy Spirit to reveal what submission is and define it specifically to your marriage. Next, you need to *"study to show yourself approved unto God"* by going into the treasury of scripture to define and learn the scriptural art of submission. Understand that as you study the word, know that scripture is a living-breathing spirit and in the natural had to be inspired by men who wrote these spiritual conducts in their native tongue. They did not write the Bible in English! Scripture must be translated from the original language into our language to give its original standard meaning— not with in our standard of understanding. Hence, when you search for the translation, you actually get the fullness of what God breathed on these individuals to interpret for us all.

Submission in Greek is: πμαι *(hupotassomai)*. Hupotassomai is a Greek word that is technically a word blend or in english a portmanteau or compound word. It comprises (tasso) with the prefix (hupo). This verb was a military term for arranging soldiers in ordered formation to confront an enemy. This also could be translated as "set," "arrange," "order," or "deploy." The grammar is important as well. The ending of the word tells you it is in the passive/middle voice. "Deploy-yourself-under." What you're observing is not an ancient Greek word for abstract obedience but a concrete metaphor of military support. Strong's is where you'll see references to commentators noting that it is "primarily military" and offering an array of possible English synonyms for that root verb:

– "/**tasso** (place in position, post) was commonly used in ancient military language for designating/appointing/commissioning a specific status..."

– "**tasso** was primarily a military term meaning 'to draw up in order, arrange in place, assign, appoint, order..."

*(See Strong's concordance #5021 for tassow: http://biblehub.com/greek/5021.htm)*

Notice, this speaks to just the tasso portion. Tasso is military strategist term and can be observed in Ephesians 5:22 as: "place yourselves under your husband." This is partially correct. Then you might look as past translators have for something like, "be subject to," in order to render the verse in better, quicker English. However, when you read this scripture in accordance to English understanding, you lose the power, meaning, revelation, and treasury of scripture. You literally miss the Commander of the Host of Heaven (Abba Father) deploying your abilities as a wife, commanding you, *hupotassomai*, which is about preparing yourself for battle and deploying or stationing yourself in support of your husband.

The phrase in which the KJV and some modern translations give "submit" for the verb "hupotassomai" is embedded within a passage that provides an extended military metaphor. In order to grasp the fullness of what Apostle Paul was saying, pay attention to the scripture closely, as scripture is not broken, not broken english, and not helter-skelter! In Ephesians 5:1-20, Apostle Paul proceeds (Ephesian 5:22) by inspiring us to forsake the "bondage" of the ways of past sinful lifestyles and fleshly nature and to take up our new lifestyle in the Spirit of Christ and (Ephesians 5:1-20) to live joyously instead in new ways, "singing and making melody...giving thanks for everything." However, Apostle Paul continues his letter about leaving the ungodly life and going in a godly lifestyle. Then he brings order to husband and wives. Lastly, Apostle Paul writes the passage (on the nature of spiritual warfare):

> *Finally, my brethren, be strong in the Lord, and in the power of his might. Put on the whole armour of God, that ye may be able to stand against the wiles of the devil. For we wrestle not against flesh and blood, but against principalities, against powers, against the rulers of the darkness of this world, against spiritual wickedness in high places. Wherefore take unto you the whole armour of God, that ye may be able to withstand in the evil day,*

> *and having done all, to stand. Stand therefore, having your loins girt about with truth, and having on the breastplate of righteousness; And your feet shod with the preparation of the gospel of peace; Above all, taking the shield of faith, wherewith ye SHALT be able to quench all the fiery darts of the wicked. And take the helmet of salvation, and the sword of the Spirit, which is the word of God: Praying always with all prayer and supplication in the Spirit, and watching thereunto with all perseverance and supplication for all saints;*
>
> — EPHESIANS 6:11-18

Ephesians chapter 6 flows straight away from chapter 5 to bring order in the house of the Lord and in the family. It is not by happenstance that Apostle Paul addresses the family and then spiritual warfare! Ephesians chapters 5 and 6 are not isolated events but a complete idea in the letter that was written to the Church of Ephesus. Additionally, Apostle Paul instructs the body of Christ on *"putting on the armour of God."* Each and every instrument of war is described with its skill, mode of use, and attributes that believers must possess and "put on." As believers, you are equipped to put on the full armour of God and deploy yourselves against the enemies of your souls. As believers you are to challenge darkness and bondage through spiritual warfare, or better, a stance of spiritual warfare in your marriages and families. That's why the writer is using military verbs like ω"tasso"("deploy" / "arrange in formation").

There are other passages in the new testament about marriage, using similar metaphors such as 1 Corinthians 7. Husbands and wives are seen as radically interdependent. In 1 Corinthians 7:4, Paul writes that each spouse yields authority to the other, using a military term for delegating power ("exousiazei"). He also says this not as a "command," as the thought is not contained within revelation, but within the mind of Apostle Paul. Then, in 1 Corinthians 7:12-16, Paul writes, when married to someone who is not a believer, the spouse should not separate the marriage due to that reason but should do all they can to support their unbelieving spouse -because God has called them to *("eirene")*. This word translates as "peace" – but it's actually different from the Roman peace, the "peace" that you  inherited in phrases like, "rest in peace" or "restfulness." It comes from the verb *eir* – to tie or weave together. The idea is that you are to be woven together. Elsewhere, in Romans, Paul asks all people to weave themselves together in love. *(For more on eirene, see Strong's #1515: http://biblehub.com/greek/1515.htm)*

In the scriptures that speak truth about interdependency and support (the era which speaks truth to our present day), Apostles in the new testament challenged the issue of believing wives with unbelieving husbands. Specifically, they challenge how to face the world together and speak your faith to a Greek or Roman husband who believes you are property (this is the topic in 1 Corinthians 7:12-16). They also challenge the need for husband and wife to put on the armor of God and resist the devil (in Ephesians 5-6). Remember that at the time, these letters were being written to challenge hierarchy, not support it, and to propose a radical equality and justice in marriages.

Moreover, most believers in first-century Eurasia were women. The teaching that you are all one body in Christ was a harder pill to swallow for men in the Roman Empire than it was for women. In the culture of that era, husbands were to own (as property) wives and rule over them. Apostle Paul writes Ephesus admonishing husbands instead to *"love your wife"* as he loves his own self (Ephesians 5); and Apostle Peter writes to treat wives as ***"joint heirs in the grace of life"*** (1 Peter 3:7). Joint heirs! The apostles challenged Roman marriages throughout the spread of conversion into salvation to walk away from harsh treatment of wives and walk on one accord! This was ludacris in that era, but it is Christ's every era!

Husbands who became believers in that first-century world are urged to love their wives and treat them as joint heirs. Wives, on the other hand, many of whom had husbands who have not converted into salvation are being encouraged to deploy themselves in support of those husbands. Unbelieving husbands are exposed to spiritual darkness and its elements. They are yoked and in bondage to sins and sinful ways of thinking and being. Apostle Paul admonishes:

> *For how do you know, wife, whether you will save your husband [by leading*
> *him to Christ]? Or how do you know, husband, whether you will save your*
> *wife [by leading her to Christ]?*

> - I CORINTHIANS 7:16 (AMP)

The Greek word for the verb "save" is *(sozo)*, meaning to rescue from destruction and bring the rescued to refuge or safety. We also draw from *(sozo)*, the word "savior."
*See Strong's #4982: http://biblehub.com/greek/4982.htm*

Keep in mind for the first century believer that there is no need to instruct wives to obey their husbands. Obedience is already an expectation in that culture. Understand that what the apostles are contending for is a radically interdependent marriage through yielding to and honoring each other. Husbands who have material power over their spouses in the Roman era are exhorted to love their wives (Ephesians 5), listen to her, "dwell with understanding" (1 Peter 3), and regard her as "joint heirs." Wives (many of whom in the early church have unconverted husbands) are encouraged to deploy themselves against "the powers of this present darkness" in support of their husbands who remain in bondage. The scriptures are not about "obedience." First-century believing women are being asked to deploy in support of their spouses because many of the spouses were unbelieving; and for believing wives of unbelieving husbands, 1 Corinthians 7 imparts instruction about not trying to convert the spouse, but instead dwell with he/she with love. And Ephesians Chapters 5-6 asserts: Stand firm against the enemy. Support your spouse in the conflict. Who knows, but through your steadfast love, they might break free?

### Scriptural Definition of Headship

But someone might ask, doesn't the next phrase after "hupotasso" talk about the husband being the head of the wife? The word used here in Greek is *"kephale."* It does mean "head." However, in English, you understand that to also mean "authority" or "leader" because head can mean both things in our language. The same is true in Latin – the word for head also means a "commander." Nevertheless, the Latin idiom (which we inherited) doesn't exist in ancient greek. Kephal in Koine Greek does have two meanings: "head" and "origin." Origin, like the head of a spring or the head of a river. A "source." Marg Mowczko summarizes some fairly extensive research documenting that it did not mean "leader" or "ruler" or anything of that kind in Greek until long after these letters were written, and you can find that summary of the research here: *https://margmowczko. com/head-kephale-does-not-mean-leader-1-corinthians-11_3/*

In the letter to the Ephesians, when calling the husband "kephale," the author may be alluding to one (or both) of the following:
* *The Hebrew lore, recorded in Genesis, that the first woman was formed from the side or rib of the first man.*
* *The logistics of Roman society by which the husband in the house is the provider and source of the house's income and resources—the bread winner. But the same word does not, by itself, mean "master." That's a different word in Greek.*

So Ephesians 5:22-23 may be saying that just as Christ is the source and the provider for the church. Husbands in Ephesus are the source of the provisions in the house. I don't think either of these two statements is a new assertion; both are stated in the text like givens that the hearers or readers already understand. The writer uses these givens as points of support for the recommendations that follow: for husbands to love (not rule) their spouses, for husbands to act sacrificially on behalf of their spouses (even as Christ does for his community), and for wives to arrange themselves, like a battle-regiment, in support of their spouses.

### Art of Submission

Apostle Paul admonishes you to understand not that the husband is boss, but that the husband in a Roman era (current times as well with an unbelieving husband) is a man that is exposed to darkness. And it's not that wives are to "obey" and "be subject" to their husbands as we have come to understand it through lost meaning. On the contrary, it is that wives are to go out to battle for their husbands' souls. The apostle's use military terms to describe the actions of wives. Instead of behaving as quiet, passive, subservient vessels and subjects of male rule, the behavior of the believing wife is the woman who issues forth in spiritual battle, dressed in *"the full armor of God,"* an agent by which Christ might "rescue" (from the verb) others on the battlefield. This is what has been buried in translation (unless searched out). The art of submission was truly lost. Submitting one to another and wives submitting to husbands has lost its vitral meaning that wives are to:

(Ephesians 5:22) "submit" or "be subject to" might be phrases like:

- "Wives, support your husbands."
- "Wives, deploy yourselves in support of your hubands."
- "Wives, arrange yourselves for battle for your husbands."

Or, less literally:
- "Wives, go to battle for your husbands."
- "Wives, defend your husbands."

(Summarized parts of article by Stant Litore *https://stantlitore. com/2018/06/25/misleading-translation-wives-submit.*)

The art of submission is to deploy yourself in battle for one's husband. When Satan is attacking you, exact spiritual warfare and might against him. Defend and go to battle on behalf of your husband, marriage, children, and lineage. When there is peace in your home, deploy your support to your spouse.

# VII

## THOU SHALT LOVE THY WIFE

*Husbands, love your wives, just as Christ also loved the church and gave Himself for her, that He might sanctify and cleanse her with the washing of water by the word, that He might present her to Himself a glorious church, not having spot or wrinkle or any such thing, but that she should be holy and without blemish. So husbands ought to love their own wives as their own bodies; he who loves his wife loves himself. For no one ever hated his own flesh, but nourishes and cherishes it, just as the Lord does the church. For we are members of His body, of His flesh and of His bones. "For this reason a man shall leave his father and mother and be joined to his wife, and the two shall become one flesh." This is a great mystery, but I speak concerning Christ and the church. Nevertheless let each one of you in particular so love his own wife as himself, and let the wife see that she respects her husband.*

- EPHESIANS 5:25-33 (NJKV)

Husbands, you are commanded to love. This job seems ineptly simple, yet for men, there is a challenge in this command that wives do not understand. Men are raised as logical, solutionists, fixers, and conquerors. Men are raised as superheroes that conquer opponents and win the girl. Husbands who are repairmen and cowboys and are solution driven eventually pull the girl onto his horse, and ride off into the sunset like television shows that become fantasies. These images drive societal messages into men outside of their soulical climate to posture themselves in the home as a conqueror or a master but not a lover. Moreover, men are rarely taught by parents and society to embrace feelings. Boys are usually told, "men, do not cry," or "stop crying; that is weak." Furthermore, men are taught that women are the feelers, and when you feel it is automatically deemed weak. Husbands must understand that lacking emotional intelligence can pull him out of oneness with his wife. Allow her to teach you emotional intelligence. Inside of her anointing you with emotional intelligence, you will learn how to properly love in accordance to God's standards and not your own, including media outlets and images.

### In Order to Love You Must Renew

Love is a spiritual substance and must be spiritually discerned. Where there is true love absent of lust, you will find God the Father:

> Beloved, let us love one another, for love is from God, and whoever loves has been born of God and knows God. Anyone who does not love does not know God, because God is love. In this the love of God was made manifest among us, that God sent his only Son into the world, so that we might live through him. In this is love, not that we have loved God but that he loved us and sent his Son to be the propitiation for our sins. Beloved, if God so loved us, we also ought to love one another. No one has ever seen God; if we love one another, God abides in us and his love is perfected in us.
>
> - I JOHN 4:7-12 (ESV)

God is love. Love is in His divine character and Him personified. Love is sacrifice, a deliberate decision, a choice, covenant, a specific place God is located in Heaven, a risk with awesome outcomes, and honest; and it is all of our english expressions [noun, verb, adjective, adverb, pronouns]. Love is eternal and cannot be stopped or dropped over trivial matters because of its unconditional and eternal nurturing nature. In contrast, lust is temporal. An argument can turn you off and never have you turned on again by this individual. Lust does have strong feelings attached. However, you can feel intense longing for this person one day and fall out of love with that same intensity the next day. As a result, men have the ability to need sex and can have sex with a woman in the absence of love. An unrenewed mind permits men to use a woman who is very well interested in them for sex. The man may or may not have any interest at all. Moreover, when a man has resentment towards his wife for perceived fussing and nagging, he has the propensity to emotionally pull away from her, not love her, but still desire sex from her. Therefore, in order for a husband to experience love, he must first renew his mind.

### *Definition of Love:*

In order to know if you are demonstrating love, we have taken 1 Corinthians 13:4-8 and broken it down so that husbands and wives understand fully what it means to lead with love.

Charity suffereth long- *Makrothymia* in Greek means that love is patient and slow to anger but not permissive; it doesn't tolerate sin, abuse, or injustice in the sense of permitting the intolerable actions and behaviors. You have the responsibility to confront them in the spirit of God's love in accordance with scripture where He "*passed in front of Moses, proclaiming, The Lord, the Lord, the compassionate and gracious God, slow to anger, abounding in love and faithfulness*" - *(Exodus 34:6, NIV).*

You also have the responsibility to walk in 1 Corinthians 13, remembering that love "*bears all things, believes all things, hopes all things, endures all things,*" and that "*love never ends*" (1 Corinthians 13:7–8).

- Kind - *chréstos,* which means "kind" in Greek, gives rise to honing a servants heart.

- Envieth not - To be jealous is one thing because it is motivated by fear, the fear that you are rivaled by someone else. However, envy is much worse! Envy speaks that the base of the motivation is murderous. Jealousy is more like, "aw man I cannot have it. That stings a bit and makes me angry." Whereas envy reads, "if I cannot have it, no one will have it; and I will take it from you." Love is not murderous. It will not steal from you or have a murderous intent towards you. Love promotes life and eternity.

- Vaunteth not itself - proudly calls attention to our possessions, our accomplishments, our associations, or our righteousness.

- Is not puffed up - Love is not prideful. It has a contrite spirit and circumcised heart; and it is both vulnerable and ready to bring fruits of repentance.

- Doth not behave itself unseemly - Is not rude, boisterous, bombastic, aggressively angry, physically violent, emotionally volatile, emotionally abusive, or verbally abusive, such as name calling and cussing each other out.

- Seeketh not her own - Love is giving and prefers others over herself. Moreover, you will be continuosly inspired to place your wife's desire, hopes, dreams, and things she wants above your own as love causes you to empty your treasury and continue to give. Love defeats selfishness!

- Is not easily provoked - Love does not easily go off. Where temptation arises to lose patience with spouse, there is nothing that your spouse will do that can emotionally

47

push you over the edge to shut down, shut them out, or produce a rash outcome after going tit-for-tat. You will not be provoked against the original assignment as husband to quit banding the house together.

- Thinketh no evil - Love does not think evil about your spouse and in return believes the best about your spouse, knowing that your spouse has your best interest at heart.

- Rejoiceth not in iniquity - Love does not rejoice in your spouses moral failures or have hidden agendas to throw their flaws and failures in their face.

- Rejoiceth in the truth - Love is a mature character standard; whereas, little boys do not like to hear or administer the truth. Contrarily, the full grown mature man knows how to receive and love the truth his wife gives him. He grows as a result and embraces his wife who is a truth teller. On the other hand, men who celebrate the truth also tell the truth, whether they are hard truths or truths to cause inspiration. "Men love truth in transparency."

- Beareth all things - Love has the ability to bear much weight and perceived stress with grace. Husbands, as the "houseband," you will feel undue pressure most of the time; however, you can withstand the weight and more with your wife and family through the character and power of love.

- Believeth all things - Love believes the best in your spouse when all options are left to believe the worst. Love has the optimism for healing and deliverance or a remedy to bring refreshing and restoration at all times.

- Hopeth all things - Love hopes continually! Hope is another nutrient from the fruit of the Spirit. Hope will have a continual expectation of the will of God over your lives even when you both cannot see it. *Hint: hope inspires the king and priest in you to rise to the occasion in your home and speak as a king with power flowing from your lips.* He is also a priest living a dual reality here on earth and in the heavenlies, readily ministering to God and carrying this inspiration back to your home.

- Endureth all things - Love has the ability to endure all things: mood swings, sickness, weakness, frailty, addictions, and such the like; and it rises to the occasion to bring deliverance and hope.

- Charity never faileth - Love never fails. This is the ultimate power of love! Because love is intrinsically eternal, it never ceases. No matter the situation or come what may, love remains strong and does not fade.

### *Lead with love*

In order for a husband to do his fullest calling unmatched in his home, he must: ***"love his wife as Christ loved the Church and gave himself for her washing her with the waters of the word to present HER (his wife) faultless unto himself,"*** which means that husbands are to be on the frontline in giving and in sanctifying. Most of us marry women and men with pre-existing conditions of trauma and dysfunction. Husbands, it is your blessed ability to wash your wife until she no longer looks like her past. When you sanctify her, you must operate in optimum love. Anytime ungodly emotions arise, you are to cleanse her and wash her over with the word to present her to yourself without issue so that she can be a wife of virtue, postured at your side to war for you and your family.

Additionally, our personal belief as to why men do not like attending church or operating in the Holy Spirit is because of an attack on the identity of the husband to keep him from maximizing his fullest potential in being the houseband and leading his home with love. Moreover, this is also where the enemy enters in with "man pride" to prevent the husband from fully embracing his role in being the first to bring Godly order, repentance, and peace into his home. Husband, receive the power to lead in the spirit of love. See your home and wife as your greatest assignment to love. Nurture, minister, and administer grace and wisdom to her with a ready word from Heaven. Use your emotional/intellectual kingly power to band your home in the direction of God's everlasting kingdom, whilst taking dominion in the things God has called you to.

# VIII

## Thou Shalt Find The Purpose Of Your Marriage

*For we are God's handiwork, created in Christ Jesus to do good works, which God prepared in advance for you to do.*

**- Ephesians 2:10 (NIV)**

*"Purpose keeps you focused on why you exist, vision aligns you with your goal, and mission empowers how you will accomplish it."*

**(Aespire.com)**

With that being said, God preordained a purpose for your marriage. This is why it is dangerous to divorce without getting a verdict from God concerning your marriage. God had something in mind when He placed you together. You did not just happen to find a fine man or a fine woman, decide to converse with them, and this one conversation led you to discover that they were the love of your life. Life and love is not that coincidental, and God did not put you together because you were so cute. He put you together for purpose—on purpose. Your marriage is a part of a greater plan that God had at work long before your mothers conceived you! So, it is your duty to find the purpose of your marriage. The purpose of your marriage answers the question, "why" God brought your marriage together in existence. Additionally, the purpose of your marriage will stand firm when all is bleak. This purpose will give you both something to fight towards on the days when you feel like the strength you have to fight for your spouse has weakened.

### *What Purpose in Your Marriage is Not*

Family, the first thing you must understand is that God did not just put you together to become parents, for parenting, for social status, or for financial gains or losses. That is not purpose. Instead, they are a bi-product of your marriage. These are all people and items that flow from the womb of your marriage, not the purpose. Your purpose is usually something that brings affectation to the world around you and influences it with the Kingdom of God. The purpose of your marriage may also feel large and unattainable based upon what God has dreamed over you before He placed you in your mothers womb. However, as long as you live, stay obedient to the Father and have a ready "yes;" in this, you both will make your purpose together, come what may!

### *How to Identify Your Purpose and What to Do With It?*

When you and your potential spouse have come to a place of liking and desiring one another, you must then begin to explore the purpose of the relationship. Now, allow this slight precursor. God is not going to give you a spiritual son or daughter to be your spouse if they are to be led to Christ by you. This individual is not your spouse. Instead, this is the lust of your heart trying to determine a role in your future, which is an alternate path that has definitive consequences involved. (2 Corinthians 6:14-18) clearly states that we do not have anything in common with those that do not believe on the same level of persuasion.

> *Do not be unequally yoked with unbelievers. For what partnership has righteousness with lawlessness? Or what fellowship has light with darkness? What accord has Christ with Belial? Or what portion does a believer share with an unbeliever? What agreement has the temple of God with idols? For we are the temple of the living God; as God said, "I will make my dwelling among them and walk among them, and I will be their God, and they shall be my people. Therefore go out from their midst, and be separate from them, says the Lord, and touch no unclean thing; then I will welcome you, and I will be a father to you, and you shall be sons and daughters to me, says the Lord Almighty.*

> - 2 CORINTHIANS 6:14-18 (ESV)

The phrase, *"do not be unequally yoked with unbelievers"* means *ápistos*. Anyone who is unfaithful in God's kingdom has attributes of being unfaithful which begets the fruit of unfaithfulness, unpersuaded, i.e. not convinced, or persuaded by God (of being in a relationship with God or God's existence). However, this does not always refer to the unconverted. John 20:21 describes someone who rejects or refuses God's inbirthings of faith and growing in the faith. With this being said, you must both be matured in the belief and dimension of faith to be properly yoked together. Being equally yoked is important if you want God to draw near to your relationship and inhabit you both. When He inhabits you both, you can release His purpose as you seek God for the purpose of your marriage. Once you and your potential determine that your relationship is heading towards marriage, you want to begin your seek in God for your collective purpose together. Be open to God's response and put to death your flesh! Begin by prayer and writing down what you both receive from God. Arrange to have premarital counseling or relationship counseling for wisdom and how to operate in application of your purpose, mission, and destiny. Next, you both should understand what your purpose is and should be energized to complete your destiny in God together. Keeping in mind your generations after you will have a culture set from the purpose God has planned for you and will feast off of your obedience for generations to come. Be a leader (king and priest) as you set examples for those after you to follow the culture of obedience to God and His purposes. You want to also teach them to be as driven or more than you. In the midst of revelation and application, minister to God, one another, and those in your spear of influence!

# IX

## Thou Shalt Have Good Communication

*"Communication is the key, as well as love; and do not try to change one another."*
— Darrell Betton (Daddy)

In marriage you must communicate! There is immense power in proper communication! Communication is paramount to the growth, development, understanding, enrichment of bonding, agreement, and godly order in the life of marriage. Communication is vital even when frustrated with your spouse. Shutting down is dangerous. You must place pressure on character weaknesses in communication that causes you to shut down (avoid) in communication out of anger or frustration, and challenge yourselves to converse with your spouse, even if you feel speechless or do not have the proper words to say. Continue to converse until both spouses have an understanding moving forward. In anger, do not just storm out of the house, go for a drive or refuse to speak. This is inevitably avoidance and running from the issue at hand. Even in the event one feels that, "if I continue to speak about this said issue it will end badly," or "my spouse cannot handle my real truth and feelings"- in that moment, inform your spouse that you need to go for a walk or a drive. Give rise to the amount of anger you have, and give a time when you will come back and continue to address the said issue. Good communication creates a healthy marriage. Conflict is healthy communication. The devil loves to play upon the thought that arguments and conflict means that the marriage is unhealthy. When you hold in anger, frustration, and unsaid communication that will assist your spouse with entering into truth, the marriage and both spouses become unhealthy.

## Good Communication

*The tongue has the power of life and death, and those who love it will eat its fruit.*
                                                        - Proverbs 18:21 (NIV)

Good communication is the sharing of thoughts, feelings, ideas, dreams, conflict, confrontation, listening, and relaying one's own ideals, hopes, and opinions. Good communication is also having a heart to understand those you communicate with and continuing conversation until you reach one mindset in comprehension. Good communicators recognize that the words spoken are creating the life you dream about or nightmares in your reality. It is important to consistently build husbands and wives!

*The wise woman builds her house, but with her own hands the foolish one tears hers down.*
                                                        - Proverbs 14:2 (NIV)

*A fool's talk brings a rod to his back, but the lips of the wise protect them.*
                                                        - Proverbs 14:4 (NIV)

Bad communication creates death, stunted growth of your marriage, and devaluation of your spouse.

Examples of bad communication reflect the following behaviors:
- Shutting down
- Being quiet when you should speak out
- Suppressing your emotions to keep peace in the marriage, getting frustrated and not talking at all
- Being passive-aggressive
- Smiling when you are upset and should be honest and assertively revealing your irritants

Other examples of bad communication are:
- blowing up and raging out aggressively to your spouse,
- icing your spouse out with the cold shoulder, and overtalking your spouse to get your point across.

Bad communication tears down the infrastructure that you have taken the time to build. Bad communication does not allow you to come into the power of oneness. Moreover, bad communication brings out division and disconnected emotions and mentality between spouses.

### Engaging Your Spouse in Disagreement

First let's discuss correcting bad ideals about arguing. Are you ready? Arguing is healthy, normal, and takes place in a Godly marriage. Additionally, there is a good communicator's way to argue. When you argue, you must fully engage your spouse. Do not behave in the following manners: shutting down and refusing to speak in the argument, getting up and escaping (leaving the argument), giving your spouse the cold shoulder, or behaving nonchalantly. Behaving like you are unaffected only causes a larger rift because you are either communicating that your spouse's feelings are unimportant or over exaggerated, or you do not care about the issue at hand. You also should not curse your spouse out (it is unloving, and you will give an account of those words that were spoken). Berating, belittling or name calling, getting physically aggressive with your spouse (men and women), or playing the avoidance game are not healthy ways of arguing. These are all bad methods of communication. When you read these methods, they look childish and bratty, right? Many times, spouses feel frustrated in arguments and stop speaking or trying to make the spouse understand what is being said. It may feel like you are running out of words or tired of talking about the same issues.

Here is the secret! Wrestle with those words. Wrestle with the frustration. Wrestle into your oneness, and communicate until you bond with your spouse. Do this until you both have understanding, are tired, and feeling emotions. Both spouses must fully engage arguments and give one hundred percent of their emotional energy, conversational power, and mentality to whatever issue is being argued about until it is no longer an issue in your marriage. Continue to press until you have healed and moved forward in your growth together! Arguments mean you are healthy, growing, and developing in your oneness! The friction (spiritual and soulical melding and binding that is tying your bond together supernaturally) of your becoming one means just that-- you are becoming one!

### *Life-giving Conversations and Hard Communications*

Confrontation, conflict, and conflict resolution are all a part of a healthy marriage. Where conflicts (arguments) are suppressed, there is usually a spouse that is being deceptive about the emotional wellbeing of the opposite spouse and perception of health in the marriage. However, there are ways to properly engage your spouse to prepare them for a confrontational conversation by warning them with: ***"This is going to be a hard conversation."*** A warning of confrontation will allow for both spouses to vent and be heard, as well as prepare the spouse to engage the conversation appropriately. On the other hand, encouraging conversations gives the opportunity to build up one's spouse, and give them "life,"—a breath of fresh air into the conversation and marital bond! Life giving conversations are building conversations. These are the conversations that cause both spouses to revisit the vision set for the marriage, recalibrate, dream again, be inspired, love deeper, and grow in intimacy and passion with one another. It's effects are freedom, pleasure, closeness, joy, and a deeper connection.

# X

## THOU SHALT KNOW THY PARTNER'S TOUCH

*I am my beloved's, and his desire is toward me.*

**- SONGS OF SOLOMON 7:10**

Each spouse has their own necessity of ministry (care, needs, desires) from the husband or wife. However, the method of ministry that each spouse has to tend to the need of one's own spouse is God's method of ministry (touch) that each spouse needs. Oftentimes, you do not understand your spouse's approach, and this misunderstanding can seem as though the spouse is uncaring, harsh, angry, too sensitive, too soft, nonchalant, pushy, numb, ambivalent, indifferent, against you, or indecisive. You have to learn to apply truth when dealing with your spouse. The truth is your spouse loves you and has your best interest at heart. Your spouse is not here to harm or hinder you but to love and inspire you. Though one spouse may be up-in-arms about a scenario and the other spouse is calm and levelheaded, does not mean the spouse is aloof or ambivalent; it is the spouse's touch (God's ministry) to you through your spouse. God uses your spouse's touch to communicate His will, power, deliverance, healing, and wholeness into your lives. God uses your spouse's touch to deliver peace where there is irrationality and love where there is turmoil.

As it pertains to learning one's spouse's touch, you must also leave room for reactions and instructions, leave room for them to be a person, and room for them to be true to themselves and their spouse. Oftentimes, you become angry because your spouse has a perceived negative reaction to information or an action when in fact the marriage is still becoming one. Your spouse is being honest within themselves and giving you blunt, truthful, or lackluster responses. Allow them to be honest and accept the spouse wholly. One may learn that you cannot attempt to change your spouse to become what you want them to be. That's called being controlling. You should not control or dominate your spouse's behavior. You cannot make them happy because you are happy. You cannot make your spouse excited because you are excited. You cannot make them mad or angry because you are angry. Some people think that having a person that always does exactly what you want is ideal. This is not ideal but rather a form of bondage. Some people feel that having a spouse who responds the same way you do would be fun and would equate to fewer fights and more peace. On the other hand, having your exact twin may just end up being boring. God intended to give you someone that is not exactly like you. God intended to give you the spice of life. That person's difference gives you unique experiences that only they can bring to the relationship.

Accept these differences and relinquish the desire to control your spouse. Having a puppet you can manipulate may seem fun for some, but this is not what marriage should look like. Accept them and the touch God is extending towards you through your spouse. Your spouse's touch allows for an open Heaven to operate freely in your lives and causes you to come into the image and likeness of God. It cleanses you. Your spouse's ministry to the base of your needs also helps you to heal, mature, grow and become complete from trauma, dysfunction, and childhood crises. Do not negate or shut down your spouse's approach to you. Do not try to change them. Just because your spouse may appear to be too gentle in times of frustration, or on the contrary, too harsh, does not mean that they must respond to situations, stimuli, and environments the way that you do. God has graced them with a different reply under certain conditions to minister to the needs that you have. Do not frustrate yourself with the task of wanting them to see the scenario the way that you do, or respond to the environment around you in the ways that you would. Simply accept your spouse for who they are and the ministry they provide in given circumstances.

# XI

## Thou Shalt Create Healthy Boundaries

*The Lord is my chosen and assigned portion, my cup; You hold and maintain my lot. The lines have fallen for me in pleasant places; yes, I have a good heritage. I will bless the Lord, Who has given me counsel; yes, my heart instructs me in the night seasons. I have set the Lord continually before me; because He is at my right hand, I shall not be moved. Therefore my heart is glad and my glory [my inner self] rejoices; my body too shall rest and confidently dwell in safety,*
**- Psalm 16:5-9 (AMP)**

Y ou must understand that boundaries are established upon goodness. Boundaries keep relationships healthy and orderly. All have an established and assigned route from the Father; however, boundaries assist you with response to invasions of your livelihood and assignment. The effect is how to properly respond to an environment that is ungodly. Boundary lines come from glory and the counsel of Heaven. They uphold a pleasant standard. Oftentimes, when your spouse and other relationships have boundaries, an ungodly nature within you will rise up to challenge or break boundaries. The nature you observe is the spirit of rebellion. Rebellion knows the proper way to go but in the end chooses to do what is wrong. We must understand that even God had boundaries.

*You shall set bounds for the people all around, saying, 'Beware that you do not go up on the mountain or touch the border of it; whoever touches the mountain shall surely be put to death. 'No hand shall touch him, but he shall surely be stoned or shot through; whether beast or man, he shall not live ' When the ram's horn sounds a long blast, they shall come up to the mountain.*

**- Exodus 19:12-13 (NASB)**

When God went to visit Moses, He placed proper boundaries around Himself to protect him and the children of Israel. Proper boundaries are not placed because you fear but because we love and protect. Boundaries that are set from a place of fear attracts demons to the situation, and the result is boundaries being broken and disrespected.

### Boundaries within marriage

There should always be healthy boundaries set within healthy marriages and relationships. Boundaries create purity. Boundaries are also established upon purity. Boundaries also hold both parties responsible and accountable for godly and ungodly activities within the marriage. Where there is no accountability within the marriage, there will be imminent danger; and where there is no responsibility, there you'll find immaturity. Boundaries also assist spouses in freedom from the bondage of controlling spirits as you recognize that you cannot control what others do or perceive as wrong or unjust. However, you can only control your actions and reactions.

When a spouse is dangerous and immature, they will not respect boundaries and attempt to either violate boundaries (break boundaries on purpose) or begin to intimidate the other spouse out of the boundary by claiming the boundary setter is being controlling. Understand, boundaries are not controlling measures but a love and protection measure. For example, if the said boundary is created stating that "if you continue to do drugs I will separate myself and the children from this environment," and then that boundary is broken (spouse continues with doing drugs), here is my reaction to the breach: the spouse has to follow through with the boundary to care for themselves and the children until the spouse has brought fruits of repentance. This is not controlling and yelling at the spouse but removing self from the equation. When boundaries are properly kept, there is purity in behavior, motivations, desires, and intentions towards spouse and self, which are stimulated and produced in action.

# XII

## Thou Shalt Not Keep Secrets

*For God will bring every deed into judgment, with every secret thing, whether good or evil.*

*- Ecclesiastes 12:14 (ESV)*

S ecrets are complete deception. Secrets are not protecting your spouse. Secrets carry lethal blows to test confidence and security. Secrets arouse the judgment of God and opens the way for the key of revelation to expose what is in hiding. The word secret is *alam* which means "hidden" in the original Hebrew. This word means to blind, disregard, escape, neglect, hidden, hidden sin, to hide from one's eyes, hides, melt, pay no attention, pretenders, secret, and to shut out. However, the definition and cross referenced scriptures give rise to a much deeper enemy working and the power of God! Secrets are toxic and are deeply spiritual in nature!

> *In pride the wicked pursue the needy; let them be caught in the schemes they devise. For the wicked man boasts in the cravings of his heart; He blesses the greedy and reviles the LORD. In his pride the wicked man does not seek Him; in all his schemes there is no God. He is secure in his ways at all times; your lofty judgments are far from him; he sneers at all his foes. He says to himself, "I will not be moved; from age to age I am free of distress." His mouth is full of cursing, deceit, a and violence; trouble and malice are under his tongue. He sits in the lurking places of the villages; In the secret places he murders the innocent; His eyes are secretly fixed on the helpless. He lies in wait secretly, as a lion in his den; He lies in wait to catch the poor; He catches the poor when he draws him into his net. So he crouches, he lies low, That the helpless may fall by his strength. He has said in his heart, "God has forgotten; He hides His face; He will never see.*
>
> *- Psalms 10:2-11 (NKJV)*

*You have set your iniquities before You, your secret sins in the light of your countenance.*

- Proverbs 90:8 (NKJV)

Proverbs 90:8 speaks of the power of God to judge and reveal secrets with the brightness of His Light, which reveals and exposes deception and darkness. Know this. God sees all, knows all, is always present, and is everywhere all at once. It is prideful to believe that God has forgotten, or is ignorant to the things that are being hidden from one's spouse. Secrets and those that commit to secrets are equated to being a manipulative murderer. How? In Psalms 10:2-11, it seems as though there is comfort in the secrecy of evildoing. A prideful one succumbs to knowing that what is hidden from the spouse is fulfilling to the flesh of eyes, nose, mouth, touch, and hearing.

Understand, secret dealings, whether it be entertaining pornography, passcodes on devices, emotional or physical adultery, pseudospouseses, addictions, inappropiate conversations, inappropiate relationships, and friendships that both spouses do not agree upon, literally kills the innocent. Secrets are destructive! Secrets produce godless environments for the enemy to drive darkness and causes the secret bearer to increase in godless appetites and pursue activities until justice is released. Secrets are entrapments that the devil uses and are oftentimes compelled through voids to receive peace from ill-gotten stress. These secrets help gain a sense of control or power, revenge, escape, the feeling of being free of responsibility and accountability, a way to self heal emotional/ mental wounds, or to break free from feeling controlled through the marriage covenant. The effect of secret keeping is killing your spouse's trust. Trust is built with consistently righteous practices; however, hiding and withholding information or lifestyle is practicing an ungodly and unsubmitted nature. Secrets are sinful and are inherently found to be under the judgment of God. When you keep secrets, you are saying to your spouse and Jesus Christ, "I am readily breaking your vows today;" and "yes, I refuse to reveal the full details to you because there is something worthy of hiding that you should be concerned about."

Secrets such as locking your spouse out of your social media accounts, extra email accounts that the spouse may or may not have knowledge about, passcodes to cell phones, notebooks, laptops, desktops, creditworthiness, bank accounts (balances, withdrawls, deposits, secret accounts because mama said to have a "little something on the side that he does not know about if he acts out," and account access), addictions, and concealing specific details that your spouse is asking of you with full disclosure. Consider God's viewpoint. When you walk in righteousness, THERE IS NOTHING TO HIDE AWAY IN DARKNESS, DECEPTION, AND LIES. When you are walking in proper fellowship with your spouse and God, you will never mind being accountable and honest. Moreover, most marrieds do not understand that when you sow little lies you reap entire darkness. They are usually not prepared for the outcome of sowing into deceptions and reaping entire abject blackness. My daddy taught that "honesty is truth in transparency." You must have full disclosure in your marriage!

# XIII

## Thou Shalt Crush Addictions

*All things are lawful for me, but not all things are helpful. All things are lawful for me, but I will not be dominated by anything.*
**- I Corinthians 6:12**

Addictions come in many forms. However, in any form they are destructive to the union and equally as harmful to the spouse. Addiction means that there is something outside of you that dominates your life, and you have become dependent upon its dominance to cope with pain in your life. Addictions come in the form of alcohol, drugs (prescription or recreational), food, exercising, weightloss, weight gain, working, eating disorders, pornography, sex, love, orgasms, gaming, shopping, spending money, and gambling. Addictions are selfish in nature. They hurt you and those who love you as it breaks down your body and soul, giving permission for the enemy to produce a death process in your life.

*For the wages of sin is death; but the gift of God is eternal life in Christ Jesus our Lord.*
**- Romans 6:23**

Addictions, act as a pseudo-salvation in the lives of those addicted. They give a sense of freedom to spend, feel good, feel healed if only for a moment, and escape trauma and dysfunction. However, there is no other escape from inner and outer turmoil than Jesus Christ.

*For whosoever calls upon the name of the Lord shall be saved.*

- Romans 10:13

The word saved in the Greek is, *"sozo"* and is defined "from a primary sos (contraction for obsolete saos, "safe"); to save, i.e. deliver or protect (literally or figuratively):--heal, preserve, save (self), do well, be (make) whole." *Strong's #4982*

### How Addictions Operate

Addictions operate through the pleasure centers of the brain and the cycle processes of the pleasure centers. This is why at certain times of the day, month or year, the drive to quench the desire increases and decreases. Addictions are perverse in nature and operate through demons of rebellion, witchcraft control, lust, and perversion. Those demons become the lord over the pleasure centers, and trigger them at the whims of old traumas, escape, and self-medicating. Jesus must become the Lord over your pleasure centers. After making Jesus Lord over your pleasure cycles, you must have the will to fight the fight of overcoming the addictions and appetites that are driven to satiate the addiction. In choosing to fight this fight, you must choose, and take ownership of your Jesus, spouse, and children.

### Addictions Break the Laws of Marriage

Addictions are rooted in selfishness and individualism. They rule the flesh through spending money and breaking your spouses permission. Generally the spouse's desire is for the addicted spouse to stop the addiction. The addicted spouse usually undermines the boundary and hides the habit. Addictions keep spouses from entering into oneness because both spouses are not in symbiotic agreement with the addiction. As a result, individualism/selfishness breaks down the marriage overtime, resulting in the following: living separate lifestyles, adultery, theft, separation, hurt, distrust, divorce, and death.

Moreover, the spouse that does not use drugs attempts to fight for control in the out of control atmosphere. The only way to operate is to, *"walk in the Spirit"* and sup on the *"Fruit of the Spirit"* which gives self-control, creating boundaries and follow through when boundaries are broken. There are no individuals in a marriage. Marriage is two people who have become one physically, financially, economically, socially, emotionally, and spiritually. And, this is the part that one would ask: "Well who am I hurting?" Here is the answer: "Everyone!" The marriage and family hurts when the addicted spouse hurts. The marriage and family suffers when monies that were allocated and agreed upon for other means are stolen to gratify selfish desires. The marriage and the family hurts when demons of addiction tread the home underfoot, and make the environment a warzone. The marriage and the family hurt when God is not lording over emotions; but the addictive highs and lows are lording over emotions, causing instability, hurt, and lost time. You must crush addictions because....

*No, in all these things we are more than conquerors through Him who loved us.*

- ROMANS 8:37 (ESV)

# XIV

## THOU SHALT HAVE ORDER

*The steps of a man are established by the LORD, when he delights in his way;*
**- PSALMS 37:23 (ESV)**

In marriage, order is a must! It is paramount in priority and should not be thrown out because of the spirit of the rebel. You can be a rebel in your own marriage, or you can be a rebel against other peoples' marriages. The rebel doesn't have a particular face, age, or demographic. The rebel is a spirit. A spirit that we often allow in. The spirit of the rebel has a huge problem with authority. Rebels are not interested in following any orders. Even when the order is good, Godly, and of sound mind. They will first challenge it or the person giving the order and then ultimately do the opposite. They will do the opposite in the daytime, at night time, in your face, or behind your back. The tendency for the rebel to do the total opposite in darkness or secret is its most scary attribute. Secrets from silver-tongued rebels that turn the hearts of those around you against you are dangerous. Watch the rebel spirit. Sweet, hot, fiery gossip, smudging, and bending the truth to make them look good are always a motive.

Keep your eyes open. The rebel will do whatever it takes to find its own path. Deep in their hearts they hardly ever can share a path. There is nothing wrong with going and doing life by yourself. However, doing life by yourself is not the purpose of marriage. Any path that avoids purpose is a path of destruction. It is important to note that while finding that tumultuous path, typically the rebel destroys the group or marriage with the least amount of order. If you are the rebel, you are killing your marriage. You cannot rebel and expect to have a successful marriage. You are quite literally tearing your marriage apart. Get help for your heart! Go get wise counsel. Then work to heal the soul of your marriage because you may have broken it. If you are not the rebel, then the first thing you must do is kneel and begin to pray. The issue is that the rebel believes with their whole heart that they are right. You won't be able to convince them of anything else. Pray for their mind. Pray for their heart to return to you and God. Pray that they receive the revelation of what has been happening. Pray against deception, lies in the mind, weak-mindedness, infiltrating contradicting thoughts, witchcraft, hexing, devils of strife, power-seeking, control, selfishness, double-mindedness, sneakiness, gossip, negative speaking, pride, and destruction.

Disorder is the root cause of dysfunction in marriage and family. The difference between disorder and dysfunction is the difference between what is happening in the soul and what is happening in the body (deeds). Disorder happens in your environment to reveal that your soul is in dysfunction. For example, a messy home is recognized with the naked eyes; however, dysfunction is happening inside of the individual that knows their home is dirty but is powerless to bring order to it. Usually you function in dysfunction as in a normal inward environment, and someone from the outside has to reveal that the conversational exchange, sex-life, and emotional instability is unhealthy. Disorder has taken root in the behaviors of depression, anxiety, hoarding, cheating, sexlessness, oversexed, fighting, bad communication, no communication, roommate behavior, and addictions. Unless the environment in the home is functional toxicity or so dysfunctional to the point that disorder is revealed, marriages continue years and years in the same disorder until someone challenges the dysfunction (children and friends).

Married couples grow old together for the kids, and when they become adults, the marriage ends. If you realize your marriage is in disorder now, you must take the power Jesus Christ has given you both to exchange the demonic power of disorder for Jesus Christ's power for order. To break the cycle of disorder and soulical dysfunction, both spouses must recognize they are both responsible and accountable for breaking this cycle. The wife cannot change for the good more than the husband, and the husband cannot change for the good more than the wife. Both spouses must acknowledge that both parties are sowing death into their own marriage. Both spouses must be intentional in the outcome of turning to God together to receive deliverance, healing, counseling, wholeness, returning to norms, happiness within oneself, and happiness together.

Godly order is necessary and simply makes sense. Godly order is the foundation on which every marriage must stand. When a marriage is out of order it breeds dysfunction. Dysfunction breeds discord. Discord breeds rebellion. Rebellion releases a supernatural level of inordinate sin. Sin breeds death. Death's manifestation in marriage is divorce. I want to make a bold statement: *"Divorce should not be an idea at all."* Divorce should be an anomaly. I would be bold to say that in the entire world, especially in America, there should be a 1% divorce rate. That means that 99% of marriages should be happy and working towards their journey in purpose and destiny. I recognize that many couples end up divorcing one another, but this should not be so! God never intended for marriage to end but through the physical death of your mate. This is God's order. This is the standard. If you believe that God is a God of order then you cannot just walk out of your marriage. The power of God's order is the power to stay. It's the power to remain. Sometimes tapping into God's order hurts. His order does not feel good all the time. God's order requires all of His people to submit to Him and His will because, His ways are higher than our ways *(Isaiah 55:9)*.

> *All the ways of a man are clean in his own eyes; but the Lord weigheth the spirits. Commit thy works unto the Lord, and thy thoughts shall be established. The Lord hath made all things for himself: yea, even the wicked for the day of evil. Every one that is proud in heart is an abomination to the Lord: though hand join in hand, he shall not be unpunished. By mercy and truth iniquity is purged: and by the fear of the Lord men depart from evil.*
>
> - PROVERBS 16:2-6

There are times when submitting to God makes you feel like you are defeated. Sometimes the feeling of losing self-respect in a relationship is spirit-crushing. However, a new thought patterning must occur. The new thought should be that you are not defeated but that you are giving it away. How about the thought that you have so much that you can now give freely. Many people become lost in their own relationships because they feel that they are always on the bottom of the stick or the losing end of the bargain. However the natural order of relationships is to give and release your mental, emotional, and physical energy into your spouse. The two must become one. Nothing in marriage is equal, but everything is relative. Understand that if one person in the marriage feels that they are losing, then both spouses are losing even if the other person doesn't see it, feel it, or display it. One is not separate from the other! Before you jump out of the boat and go on some epic journey to find yourself again because you feel like you are giving too much away, please consider that your spouse may feel and give the same amount that you do to the relationship, family, and business welfare of your last name. Please consider they are sacrificing and working as well. They may be working in a different way than what you feel is right, but they are still working towards both of your goals. You cannot control them and make them do everything you want and when you want them to do it. That's not Godly order. That's called domination or enslavement. You also do not want to be the one having a hissy fit every time things don't go your way. That is called being a brat. Let go freely and give into your relationship the same way that God did. God gave his best. God gave Himself... Jesus! And to top it off, God thought you were worth it with all the less than perfect ways you can be sometimes. Your spouse is worth you giving everything! This is order.

Thou shalt have order. Thou shalt have order in your family, job, finances, church service, and fun time. You cannot have order without priorities. Priorities are a byproduct of order. For example, you never want to put the church in front of your wife. Why? Because eventually, your marriage will fail. You never want to put fun time in front of financial order because eventually you will run out of finances and may end up homeless. There is nothing worse than the lights getting turned off because you used the electric bill money for that new gaming system or that new pair of expensive shoes. Every time priorities and order are ignored destruction and poverty follow.

Setting order in your life is truly the fastest way to go from regular to extraordinary. Setting your priorities is what keeps you in order. Order is a mental training of living good principles. However, when you set your priorities, you set your heart's standards. When your heart, mind, belief, and behavioral patterns line up, then the order of

God is established. There is absolutely nothing in this world that can stop the power of God when people are enacting His order and sovereign rule. A man or woman in order is equivalent to God's force on the earth. When you know the order of family, then you can set priorities in your life decisions. Any man or woman that does not understand the order of the family is dangerous to themselves and those around them. The order of the family begins with God. Both the man and woman must acknowledge God first if they want His covering.

> And thou shalt love the LORD thy God with all thine heart, and with all thy soul, and with all thy might.
>
> - DEUTERONOMY 6:5

This command from the bible places God as the priority. He is first in order. He is also first in priority. He is first in all things. Worship and love to the Lord are not to be confused with service to the church and assembly of believers. This type of service is subsequently down the line of more important priorities that God wants to set into your life. Secondly, the next order of family goes to those that are married. If you are married, then every priority under God points to your spouse as next in the priority of life. Anytime a married couple places someone, something, or some event in front of the marriage covenant, it is like worshipping some strange demi-god and then asking the Lord of lords if it is okay. It is like having sex with 100 other women or men and then asking the one you married if it is okay. In both cases, the answers to both questions should be common sense. It is and will always be an adamant no! No, it is not okay. Just as God says He would have no graven images before Him, it is not okay. Just as God said He is a jealous God, your spouse is a jealous spouse made in the image of the almighty God. Just as your spouse is a jealous spouse, they demand priority.

This priority in the spectrum of life and Godliness is number two, being only second to God Himself. So if you are preferring a friend, you are out of order. If you prefer the job or business before your spouse, you are out of order. Please don't say you are doing 90-120 hours a week for them (your spouse) if they disagree or if they call you home, and you choose not to go home. You are out of order. If you are preferring your mommy or daddy over your spouse, you are out of order. Mommy and daddy came together and gave birth to you so you may feel that you owe them a huge debt; however, any debt you owe them cannot be placed higher than the debt of commitment and promise you made before God, Heaven, Earth, the priest, family members, and your spouse. No matter how you feel, you must act, execute, and perform on behalf of your spouse before any and all parents, aunts, uncles, brothers, sisters, sons, daughters, friends, and associates. When you said, *"I do,"* you said that you would *"forsake"* all others. (Genesis 2:24).

> *Therefore a man shall leave his father and his mother and hold fast to his wife, and they shall become one flesh.*
>
> - GENESIS 2:24 (ESV)

As a husband, Paul states in Ephesians to *"love our wives just as Jesus loves the church and gave himself up for it.* (Ephesians 5:25)

> *Giving thanks always for all things unto God and the Father in the name of our Lord Jesus Christ; Submitting yourselves one to another in the fear of God. Wives, submit yourselves unto your own husbands, as unto the Lord. For the husband is the head of the wife, even as Christ is the head of the church: and he is the savior of the body. Therefore as the church is subject unto Christ, so let the wives be to their own husbands in everything. Husbands, love your wives, even as Christ also loved the church, and gave himself for it;*
>
> - EPHESIANS 5:20-25

In this line of scripture, God begins by telling both husband and wife to submit to each other. This is truly the wisdom of the Lord. One is not greater than the other as it resolves to respect and worship to the Lord. However, on the next line, God gives order as to how to behave in the marriage union. Wives are to submit to their own husbands. Then God places the husband as head of the wife like God is head of the church. God places serving your husband in submission on the same level as serving God. Equivalent to the church's submission to Christ. As you can see there is an interweaving and locking of order, command, submission, and love in the marriage union. God commands husbands to love their wives so much that they would do anything and be willing to give their life for their wives. God commands wives to submit to their husbands as though they are submitting to God Himself. This is a high command. This is the order of God. This order resets and fixes the Adam and Eve debacle. When you live by this order, the blood of Jesus actually cleanses those that are married from the curse since Adam and Eve disobeyed. If you are not living by the new promise in God then you and your marriage are living by the old curse.

Next in the precession of order in God's family unit are the children. Both the husband and the wife will become one, and from this oneness will come children. The children are a by-product of a healthy sexual relationship between husband and wife. Children are not an inconvenience or a burden. Children are not to be rejected or regretted, but every child should be celebrated and raised in the admonition of the Lord.

*Children, obey your parents in the Lord, for this is right. "Honor your father and mother" (this is the first commandment with a promise), "that it may go well with you and that you may live long in the land." Fathers, do not provoke your children to anger, but bring them up in the discipline and instruction of the Lord.*
*- Ephesians 6:1-4 (ESV)*

*Direct your children onto the right path, and when they are older, they will not leave it.*
                                                    - PROVERBS 22:6 (NLT)

Do not raise your child without a deep and intimate relationship with God. Not having a relationship with God will quite naturally condemn the generations. It also sets the child up to be rebellious to the Lord, their parents, and other authority figures. God is the number one need for children. God is the number one priority for your child's life. Teaching your child to love, worship, and walk with God is the peak of parenting. Over the years you will have confidence knowing that they will turn out to be amazing individuals. Next in the hierarchy are your actual parents. If you are married, your parents come after taking care of your spouse, and children. Needless to say, God believes in adult children taking care of their parents.

The Bible records in 1 TIMOTHY 5:8 (ESV): *"But if anyone does not provide for his relatives, and especially for members of his household, he has denied the faith and is worse than an unbeliever."*

Take care of your parents if you have the means. After taking care of your parents, then comes your brothers and sisters and extended family in priority. Finally, the priority goes to those that are in the household of faith; and then after that, those that you may serve in the world.

GALATIANS 6:10 states: *"As we have therefore opportunity, let us do good unto all men, especially unto them who are of the household of faith."*

This scripture opens the door to serve those in the house of the Lord and those that occupy the world. But again, God gives us order. The priority in this scripture is service to the Church. It is great to go throughout the world being charitable, but it is still out of order if you have not given that same level of charity or more to the church or body of believers. This is order. It is important to note that God's largest priorities have some of the most intricate spectrums of order. God is truly a great God and he has set order so that we would not fall into destruction, deception, or self-sabotage. It is so easy to believe that one is doing the right thing when they've set out to do it. Especially when this thing seems like it will do a world of good. What you have come to know is that doing the right thing out of order is entirely the wrong thing.

# XV

## Thou Shalt Have Financial Fidelity

*And he said also unto his disciples, There was a certain rich man, which had a steward;
and the same was accused unto him that he had wasted his goods. And he called him, and
said unto him, How is it that I hear this of thee? give an account of thy stewardship; for
thou mayest be no longer steward. Then the steward said within himself, What shall I do?
for my lord taketh away from me the stewardship: I cannot dig; to beg I am ashamed. I am
resolved what to do, that, when I am put out of the stewardship, they may receive me into
their houses. So he called every one of his lord's debtors unto him, and said unto the first,
How much owest thou unto my lord? And he said, An hundred measures of oil. And he said
unto him, Take thy bill, and sit down quickly, and write fifty. Then said he to another,
And how much owest thou? And he said, An hundred measures of wheat. And he said
unto him, Take thy bill, and write fourscore. And the lord commended the unjust steward,
because he had done wisely: for the children of this world are in their generation wiser
than the children of light. And I say unto you, Make to yourselves friends of the mammon
of unrighteousness; that, when ye fail, they may receive you into everlasting habitations.
He that is faithful in that which is least is faithful also in much: and he that is unjust in
the least is unjust also in much. If therefore ye have not been faithful in the unrighteous
mammon, who will commit to your trust the true riches? And if ye have not been faithful in
that which is another man's, who shall give you that which is your own? No servant can
serve two masters: for either he will hate the one, and love the other; or else he will hold to
the one, and despise the other. Ye cannot serve God and mammon. And the Pharisees also,
who were covetous, heard all these things: and they derided him. And he said unto them, Ye
are they which justify yourselves before men; but God knoweth your hearts: for that which is
highly esteemed among men is abomination in the sight of God. The law and the prophets
were until John: since that time the kingdom of God is preached, and every man presseth
into it. And it is easier for heaven and earth to pass, than one tittle of the law to fail.*
- Luke 16:1-17 (NKJV)

The aforementioned scripture in Luke chapter 16
observes that a wealthy man hads a heart of an
infidel as it pertains to monies and business dealings.
In marriage, you must not be the spouse that demonstrates
infidelity with the monies and unethical business matters.
This speaks of the business of your household bills and

running from bill collectors or illegitimate business dealings as business owners. Usually in marriage you have the spender and the saver. However, there should be honor between both spouses. It is theft to just take money and allocate it at a personal desire or whim, even if it is noble such as paying bills. Both spouses must be in agreement in the stewardship of the monies. Both spouses should have knowledge of accounts, where the monies are allocated, and how it is spent.

Do not allow Mammon (the god of substance, i.e. cars, houses, clothes, jewelry, shoes, and money) to become the lord over your home. This is dangerous. When one spouse makes mammon the lord of the home, a contentious environment in the home is created as disagreements and resentment will persist. Why? Bad stewardship and mismanagement of funds accompanies mammon. One spouse will be literally dishonest with the spending habits, overspending important and unimportant money, and placing the bills and family in harm's way with bad stewardship. Then the other spouse will be found attempting to take control of the situation in their own strength and intellect to "save" the home from perceived imminent danger. Both spouses are now in the land of flesh, hiding money like the bad steward, overspending and wasting money like the bad steward, which will lead to shrewd dealings with money and substance to stay afloat.

### Monetary Fidelity

Financial fidelity looks like all spending is open and bare for both spouses to see. Both spouses give an account for where the money is being allocated through receipts, bank statements and prior conversations. In addition, create a monthly, yearly, and weekly budget; and vision cast for your marriage to set the tone as to where, when, and how the monies and finances will be spent and allocated. Budgeting is not control! Budgeting brings accountability to both spouses. Budgeting will ensure that before extra monies are being spent for desires, that both spouses are in agreement with the purchase. Agreement brings peace into your home and reaffirms that Holy Spirit is there. To be financially honest, bank accounts must have names of both spouses on each account! There should never be a time where money is hidden. That is called financial cheating!

Moreover, hiding money is dishonest and abusive! Both spouses must have the ability to trust where the money is being allocated. When you share accounts, both should be able to see them. It brings peace into the midst when both spouses can see where the monies are going. There is no, "this is my money," or "since I am the one working, this is not your money; and you have no say in where the monies go." There is also no, "you do not have any rights to the money." These statements are the helm of financial abuse and it's unloving! There should never be a time when one spouse controls the money more than the other. Monies in a marriage is a joint venture with joint consent. This means if one spouse controls the monies and the other spouse does not have equal access to see the monies, the spirit of witchcraft control has entered into your monetary life. At that point, it is harder to keep currency flowing in your home because it is no longer God's money you are jointly stewarding, but its owner is the kingdom of Babylon and demons of Babylon who have an entire network of ways to keep you and your spouse chasing money to spend. You also are forced to work many hours a day while never clenching financial goals.

### Give Your First-Fruits Together

> The point is this: whoever sows sparingly will also reap sparingly, and whoever sows bountifully will also reap bountifully. Each one must give as he has decided in his heart, not reluctantly or under compulsion, for God loves a cheerful giver.
>
> - II CORINTHIANS 9:6-7 (ESV)

Giving to your local church should always be the epicenter of your pay week. Both spouses should jump up, gleefully, holding hands in preparation to give to God! Giving is a principle in the earth, much like seedtime and harvest time. The more you give, the more space you have for God to infuse you spiritually, naturally, and financially. Whenever you get into a space of withholding the fullness of your gifts, you have entered into dangerous grounds; and let's be honest, a disrespectful ground. You refuse to give or give your best to God in His prearranged principles toward us. Then you get into a financial crunch and pray for God to get you and your home out of the woes. That behavior is immature and lacks Godly character! If the church embraced this principle of giving, everyone would understand that this is your own personal line of future protection to insure boundless blessings and overflow in the lives of your home and lineage.

## *Stewardship*

> *But if any provide not for his own, and specially for those of his own house, he hath denied the faith, and is worse than an infidel.*
>
> - I TIMOTHY 5:8

Husbands and wives must understand that the increase you receive, i.e. possessions, monies, children, and influence are from Heaven. You must steward well over the resources of Heaven! Steward well over the resources of time, talent, and treasure. You are benefactors of Heaven to allot properly to each of the particular areas.

> *So teach us to number our days that we may get a heart of wisdom.*
>
> - PSALM 90:12 (ESV)

*Time:*

Knowing how to manage your time with your spouse, children, career, responsibilities, and rest teaches you wisdom. It will reveal what is lasting, relationships that are of importance, and how to place value systems upon this release of wisdom. This will teach you how to value and cherish what God has given you. Another important nugget is wisdom in stewarding well over your time. This places you in the promise of keeping the *"Law of Priority."*

> *For the kingdom of Heaven is as a man travelling into a far country, who called his own servants, and delivered unto them his goods. And unto one he gave five talents, to another two, and to another one; to every man according to his several ability; and straightway took his journey. Then he that had received the five talents went and traded with the same, and made them other five talents. And likewise he that had received two, he also gained other two. But he that had received one went and digged in the earth, and hid his lord's money. After a long time the lord of those servants cometh, and reckoneth with them. And so he that had received five talents came and brought other five talents, saying, Lord, thou deliveredst unto me five talents: behold, I have gained beside them five talents more. His lord said unto him, Well done, thou good and faithful servant: thou hast been faithful over a few things, I will make thee ruler over many things: enter thou into the joy of thy lord. He also that had received two talents came and said, Lord, thou deliveredst unto me two talents: behold, I have gained two other talents beside them. His lord said unto him, Well done, good and faithful servant; thou hast been faithful over a few things, I will make thee ruler over many things: enter thou into the joy of thy lord. Then he which had received the one talent came and said, Lord, I knew thee that thou art an hard man, reaping where thou hast not sown, and gathering where thou hast not strawed: And I was afraid, and went and hid thy talent in the earth: lo, there thou hast that is thine. His lord answered and said unto him, Thou wicked and slothful servant, thou knewest that I reap where I sowed not, and gather where I have not strawed: Thou oughtest therefore to have put my money to the exchangers, and then at my coming I should have received mine own with usury. Take therefore the talent from him, and give it unto him which hath ten talents. For unto every one that hath shall be given, and he shall have abundance: but from him that hath not shall be taken away even that which he hath. And cast ye the unprofitable servant into outer darkness: there shall be weeping and gnashing of teeth.*
>
> - MATTHEW 25: 14-30

### Talent:

Talent in Greek is *alanton,* which means a balance, that which is weighed, a talent (about 3000 shekels in weight) usage: a talent of silver or gold. A silver talent was worth about 6,000 denarii and gold talents were worth about 30 times as much. A talent was not a coin but rather a weight (about 75 lbs, NIVSB) used as the basis of monetary exchange. ["A talent refers to a talent-weight of silver (the weight and the value being different in different countries and at different times). A common value of a talent was 6000 denarii" (Souter).] Talent is also defined as, "that which is weighed, a talent, a. a weight, varying in different places and times also as charisma, genius and talent."

In summation, Jesus is dealing with the lack of stewardship of the talents or things stored inside of us that produce money, influence, and power from Heaven! Pay attention to the aforementioned scripture where each investee states: *"Lord the talent you deliverest unto me;"* which means your talents are not yours. Your talent is indeed the Lord's. You just steward it. You are to make good on Heaven's investment inside of you and multiply it! Do not bankrupt yourself in your talents; research, educate, and train to maximize your gifts from heaven. Make them weighty within you as you extend outward to others! Jesus is looking for his investment back from you, your spouse, and your legacy!

*For where your treasure is, there will your heart be also.*

- Luke 12:34

### Treasure:

In Greek, treasure is *thésauros* and means a store-house for precious things; hence: a treasure, a store. a store-house for precious things; hence: a treasure, a store or a receptacle for valuables. Whatever you and your spouse place high in priority and principle will become a treasure in your marriage, life, and legacy. Disclaimer: treasure can become either negative or positive based upon its inspiration, proximity to God, His standard of holiness, and agreement between spouses about the possession of the particular treasures. You must steward well over what your home stores in your hearts, in the minds, and in the vaults of Heaven. The vaults of Heaven stores treasures over you; therefore, what you esteem highly will be what your home and legacy shall receive.

# XVI

## Thou Shalt Not Be Petty

*Therefore all things whatsoever ye would that men should do to you: do ye even so to them: for this is the law and the prophets.*

- Matthew 7:12

In all marriages, there will be a temptation to be spiteful and petty. This is in the form of not accepting responsibility for disappointment, moral failure, and missing the mark by forgetting details or deciding not to do what is asked of you. However, when faced with pushback from your spouse, do not go into blaming back and forwards or playing tit-for-tat. Accept what is being said. Sit in it. Deal with it, and heal it. Do not be spiteful with your spouse to punish them back for wrongdoing. Instead, learn to accept your part in the wrongdoing. This Godly character will teach you to treat your spouse as you want to be treated, while also teaching them how to treat you!

One of the priorities in marriage is to serve. Let me say that again. Serve your spouse. When you wake up, and throughout the day, you should have careful thought on how to serve your spouse. If you have been together for any real length of time, you will begin to truly understand your spouse. You will know them better than anyone else in the world. You will know what they need and exactly what they want out of life. More importantly, you will know what they need and want from you. Being petty is deciding in your heart that you will not give your spouse what they need. Being petty is choosing that you will not fulfill anything asked of you. Why would you do this? Here is a great example of pure pettiness in action. You wake up in the morning feeling quite amazing. You think to yourself, "I could go for some good breakfast. Eggs, grits, toast, and some coffee sounds good." So, you pull out your skillet, and magically next to the eggs there is some sausage. You are ecstatic! Just the extra thing you need this morning. You start whipping the eggs. You throw the bread in the toaster, and then you think, "I could get my spouse some breakfast." Here is where the pettiness comes in. Immediately, as you have the thought to serve your spouse in bed an overwhelming thought plays out in your head, "why should I do this extra work for them, and they couldn't even talk to me yesterday?" Another thought intrudes. "The night before when I tried to make love to them, they acted like they were not in the mood and just turned over." Then another thought. "They are just so lazy. They never clean up or do anything. They don't deserve any eggs!" The final thought hits your mind and says, "would they wake up and make me a whole breakfast?" This is demonic bombardment!

Negative thoughts will create negative feelings. Negative feelings are from negative belief systems called strongholds. It is important to note that all the thoughts that are flowing through your mind are not the responsibility of your spouse. In fact, your spouse has no idea what is happening in your mind. In this example, your spouse is simply sleeping in bed. If you could reset everything, would your spouse have earned these thoughts arrowed against them? If you love them, do they deserve to have this level of assault? They cannot even hear this nor can they fight against it. The only person that has the power to deal with what is happening in your mind is you. You may say that if they had done all the opposite of what ticked you off then you would not have these thoughts nor feelings. Well, if you want to be honest and truthful then I will be brutally honest. The idea of your spouse doing everything right or what makes you happy so that you do not get so upset with them is a weak-minded, handicapping thought process which leverages spite, revenge, bitterness, resentment, and ultimately abuse into the relationship.

Your spouse right now is still lying in the bedroom. Why wouldn't you simply throw in the extra piece of toast, sausage, and eggs for them? Do they deserve punishment? Somewhere in your mind, you do not want them happy because you are not happy. You are not mad at them. You are mad at your experience of them in the past and present time. But really consider, "how are they really the reason for your anger." If the anger is long-lasting then you really need to check your heart for the answer. Most times, it has nothing to do with the person you are taking it all out on but someone who took advantage of you in your past. Does your spouse deserve to be the bag that holds all of your punishment? Do they deserve your undying wrath? Are you enacting the judgment of the Lord upon them? Do they need all of this? The short answer is no. No, your wife or husband does not deserve all the worse things in life. They do not deserve to have a hex or curse from their spouse following them day in and day out. They do not deserve pain. Even if you are in pain, it does not justify you dishing it out. Even if you are disappointed, this does not justify you proverbially kicking the dog. You having internal issues going on does not mean that other people deserve to feel the pain or embrace the negative atmosphere that you may purposely create.

Your spouse deserves the best of you. Your spouse deserves your best gift, your best talent, and your best love. Your spouse deserves the best you that you can be. Your spouse deserves the best love-making, the best of you financially, the best of you spiritually, the best of you emotionally, and the best of your will and intentions. Your spouse deserves your best effort in every facet of life. If you are not giving them your best then you are giving them your worst. This should be your new mindset and mantra. Great marriages that have great spouses don't accept an average output. Be your best self so that you can serve your best spouse.

Now, you are not a victim. Your mind and emotions are not broken. You may have been invaded by some evil thoughts, but it is up to you to determine if they should translate into evil feelings. The truth is that you are in control of your emotions. No other person is in charge of how you feel. No other person gets to determine your perspective about what has happened, or what is happening in your life. You are in charge. That person that did something to you is not in control of what you do back to them. Life in its fullness should not be an eye for an eye and a tooth for a tooth. This pettiness is truly the pride of the whole world. Having a "get you back" spirit will not better your marriage. It will not teach the best lessons and get people where they need to be. The payback mindset will not put people in their place. It does not do anything well. You cannot fight with fire. All you will have is a lot of fire and destruction. Pettiness is the spirit of pain, destruction, and control. Going tit- for-tat so that the other person will get right or finally see is not effective communication. This is not effective problem solving either. It is simply a control move. Controlling marriages are always wedged between a rock and a hard place because one person or both persons are trying to hold all the cards, and distribution of power to whom has a lower station than themselves. While on the other side, one of the spouses has to battle to decide if they should fight for position, power, authority, and freedom; or be simple, painfully lay down, and let them win. Control tries to leverage power through low self-esteem. The person with the lowest self-esteem has to platform their power and station higher to make up for what is missing. Eviscerating one spouse to empower the other is foolishness before God and much like self-mutilation because you are one.

> *Husbands, in the same way, be considerate as you live with your wives and treat them with respect as the weaker partner and as heirs with you of the gracious gift of life, so that nothing will hinder your prayers.*
>
> - I Peter 3:7 (NIV)

## *Suffering for Doing Good*

> *Finally, all of you, be like-minded, be sympathetic, love one another, be compassionate and humble. Do not repay evil with evil or insult with insult. On the contrary, repay evil with blessing, because to this you were called so that you may inherit a blessing. For, "Whoever would love life and see good days must keep their tongue from evil and their lips from deceitful speech. They must turn from evil and do good; they must seek peace and pursue it. For the eyes of the Lord are on the righteous and his ears are attentive to their prayer, but the face of the Lord is against those who do evil.*
>
> - I Peter 3:8-12 (NIV)

Getting someone back because of lying, cheating, stealing, damaged property, rape, molestation, or intimidation does not make you the better person, nor does it clear either person's wrongdoing. That is simply called revenge. Revenge does not fix problems. Revenge does not bring transformation into either person's life. Revenge does not fill the place of that which is missing. Revenge hardly ever changes the victim's true feelings or the aggressor's true feelings. Revenge is reserved for God alone. The truth is that your heart has to be cold to think about how to exercise your vengeance on your spouse. Revenge again does not solve anything by our human means.

Now here's a deep question: Does your spouse ultimately want your life to be full of misery or vice versa? If they or you do, why? Can you fix it? If you can fix it with your spouse you must do it by any means necessary. Trust God and partner with Him to repair your marriage. This really begins with having the boldness to say what really hurt you. It takes being vulnerable. The other spouse has to let down their defenses to simply listen and give comfort or a pleasing answer to the problem. Please consider that people have held grudges for decades. Wars have been incited and elevated because of having a payback mindset. War is bloody and devastating. Imagine having a war with your spouse. Should you war with your spouse? Unfortunately, petty and offended mindsets will seek to continue forward in strife and bitterness. They will say to themselves, "this person does not deserve the whole breakfast at all!"

Now is the time to change your life. Nothing will ever get better staying the same. Decide that you both are worth the best. Decide that you want an "Unbreakable Marriage." Begin by changing and relent by serving! Start the momentum! True love is worth every sacrifice. Lay down any and all pride. Let your heart, mind, will, intentions, and behaviors follow the command, "THOU SHALT NOT BE PETTY."

# XVII

## THOU SHALT NOT COMMIT ADULTERY

*Thou shalt not commit adultery.*
**- Exodus 20:14 (KJV)**

The problem with adultery is not just the feeling of betrayal. The reality of adultery is that an extra party has been brought into your most intimate space. This is a vulnerable place in your spouse's mind, emotions, will, heart, and body. This extra person, without the permission of your spouse, is hidden in a place of deception. This individual has gone where no other individual is supposed to go, has seen what they were never legally or spiritually allowed to see, and has touched what was (holy) wholly for your spouse. Then there is the issue of transgressing your vows.

> *And don't you realize that if a man joins himself to a prostitute, he becomes one body with her? For the Scriptures say, "The two are united into one."*
>
> - I CORINTHIANS 6:16 (NLT)

### Illegally Tangled

Another issue of commiting adultery, whether husband or wife, is that it's theft. An individual without permission selfishly joins themself with your spouse in an adultery entanglement. In essence, not only is the affair spouse tied to the strange man/woman, but the "innocent" spouse is tied in becoming one with the adultery without their permission. All three parties become one. Why? The husband and wife have become one. *"And, the two shall become one flesh."* Then the affair spouse has sex or an emotional bond that infringes upon the marriage and becomes one with both spouses spiritually and naturally. This is why in one moment the affair spouse will blink and hear the sound (words) of the spouse or the affair partner; and seemingly the strange man/woman and spouse begin having many similarities. It is because everyone is—one!

Additionally, once discovered, the "innocent" spouse will then become weary with wanting to find out more about the strange man/woman to the injury of seeing there are similarities. In order to break the similarities, the strange man and woman must be spiritually and naturally removed from the marriage bond. This is going to be a process of steady renewing of the mind and self-denial.

> *Then Jesus said to His disciples, "If anyone desires to come after Me, let him deny himself, and take up his cross, and follow Me."*
>
> - Matthew 16:24 (NKJV)

Self-denial looks like this scripture:

> *For though we walk in the flesh, we do not war according to the flesh. For the weapons of our warfare are not carnal but mighty in God for pulling down strongholds, casting down arguments and every high thing that exalts itself against the knowledge of God, bringing every thought into captivity to the obedience of Christ.*
>
> - II Corinthians 10:3-5 (NKJV)

The natural work that must be done for self-denial and going after Christ looks like every thought about the strange man/woman must being brought to the conviction of Christ Jesus. Every flashback must be condemned in spiritual warfare. The spouse must have a made up mind that affairs will never happen again by cutting off all communication with the strange man/woman. You must also have open honest conversations with your spouse to heal and not injure. Allow your spouse to vent the frustrations about any hurt and betrayal in honesty without retort and be consistent in character with honor, truth, and justice. All things secret must be laid bare (passwords, devices, locations, etc.), and reaffirm your life in Christ Jesus. Is all of this a spirit of control or is this controlling your spouse? The answer is no! They lost control and needed accountability and truth to deny oneself in place of secrecy and idolatry. Moreover, as both spouses heal and remove the strange man or woman out of the marriage bond, (the twaining of the two) it will become easier to not be drawn to the strange man/woman. Longing for the strange man or woman will cease, and being accountable will no longer be an issue.

### Mental Binding

In order to have an affair, there are a series of mental bondages that the enemy uses before he attacks your pleasure centers. First, the enemy begins with mind-control to begin lusting after men or women in your heart. This longing coupled with the pressures of your home, life, and past rejection and abandonment starts the mind binding process. Mind binding is where the enemy of your soul creates outlets and excuses to have the affair and brings in issues to create a false legality to have the affair. In this position you will find strongholds and arguments against the spouse in the spirit. The enemy is attempting to establish adultery in the marriage over, "Mary is against you." "I am always wrong;" or "John is not attracted to you any longer. You may as well get what you deserve;" or "I am just tired of how this marriage is going. I need something new in my life;" or "I am too hurt. I need comfort, and my spouse is not providing the comfort that I need." Once this argument is set, the enemy sets up opportunities with co-workers, friends, passerbys, and the like; and then the soulical entanglements begin. The worst part of the enemy's trap is that you may feel like this is just a one time occasion. Before you know it, the oppression is so strong that it becomes too hard to leave the affair person alone; and the affair itself becomes an addiction. Meanwhile, your spouse is the wiser and feels the disconnection as well as the presence of an extra person in the spirit of your marriage. Additionally, the mental binding goes both ways because the innocent spouse is now attacked in their self-esteem, identity, and confidence in the marriage.

### Breaking the Power of Adultery

Both spouses must be willing to FIGHT to restore their union. First, after the D-day, both spouses must come into agreement to send the strange woman or strange man away, forever. All communication with affair partner must be completely severed. No, you cannot be friends. No, they cannot call you. Not ever. Once, you have seen someone in all of their naked glory and have "gone beyond the veil," there is no longer any friendship! Next, once you have both decided to fight for your marriage, do not be prideful, and "fix it on your own." Go and get counseling! Have an outside party deal with your souls and the soul of your marriage. This is so important because if you have had a moral failure such as this, there are specific steps of soulical illness and mind binding that got the marriage to this place; and this mindset is depraved. Outside help will bring you to health and break the cycle of unhealhty, toxic, and dysfunctional cycles that your marriage has experienced. Thirdly, be patient. Your spouse is a person, and you both will have to learn to truly accept them in the healing process. The one who broke the marriage will be the one God uses to heal the marriage. Further, the innocent spouse has to accept the ministry and change from the spouse that is healing the union. Additionally, the affair spouse has to accept the emotions of the innocent spouse. All of their emotional trauma and questions. No, your spouse will not just, "get over it." Emotions and healing does not work like that. Lastly, rebuild trust! Rebuilding trust is difficult. You will both have to be humble and share passwords, locations on devices, and be consistent in character at all times. Wherever you say you are going to be and the time you said you will return, must be exact and accountable for all outings. Moreover, you must PRAY together! Pray and believe in God for the complete restoration of your marriage. This process takes a lot of humility and responsibility; however, *All things are possible with God*" and your marriage can be saved!

# XVIII

## THOU SHALT LIVE SAVED TOGETHER

*Therefore if there is any consolation in Christ, if any comfort of love, if any fellowship of the Spirit, if any affection and mercy, fulfill my joy by being like-minded, having the same love, being of one accord, of one mind. Let nothing be done through selfish ambition or conceit, but in lowliness of mind let each esteem others better than himself. Let each of you look out not only for his own interests, but also for the interests of others.*
### - PHILIPPIANS 2:1-4 (NKJV)

Sometimes both spouses start their journey together before engaging in a personal relationship with Jesus. Oftentimes, one spouse will get saved while the other is proverbially dragging their feet in the valley of decision. For the spouse that is worried that their lover is unsaved or a "non practicing Christian," there is scriptural relief.

> *For the unbelieving husband is sanctified by the wife, and the unbelieving wife is sanctified by the husband; otherwise your children would be unclean, but now they are holy.*
>
> ### - I CORINTHIANS 7:14

The treasure of this scripture is revealing just how powerful and covenantal your relationship with Christ and the oneness is in your marriage. It is beautiful that God would allow the saved spouse to live in a way that cleanses the unbelieving spouse.

Moreover, as you live upright, the power is that your spouse will receive salvation as the pull for holiness and drawing power of the Holy Spirit will do the "convicting of sin." The power of the Holy Spirit will pull your spouse's desires for Christ into the body of Christ. It is unscriptural to up and divorce your spouse because they are not accepting Jesus as their personal Lord and Savior. The spirit of control does not make it conducive for the Holy Spirit to draw your spouse. Instead, it creates an environment of disunity and strife. Additionally, it is erroneous to advise a believer to leave their spouse over lack of salvation.

> *And if a woman has an unbelieving husband and he is willing to live with her, she must not divorce him.*
>
> - I CORINTHIANS 7:13 (BSB)

The spirit of error and witchcraft that advises the sanctifying spouse to leave the unbelieving spouse must leave out of the Church. Here is an audacious statement…. I hope you are ready! If your spouse remains unwilling to accept your religious relationship with Christ or accept Him as their personal Lord and Savior, then it is time for you to check the climate of your relationship in Christ. If you are saved, your character is to strive to live in peace with everyone whether saved or not. Yes, scripture validates walking in agreement with light and light bearing relationships. However, that does not mean treating those who have not accepted Jesus with contempt. This behavior is the spirit of religion and tradition at work and it's keeping you from experiencing the fullness of Christ. These spirits operate to keep you and your spouse outside of Christ so the atmosphere is contemptible in your home.

I dare say, if your spouse remains unsaved around you who claims salvation, where is your Jesus? Is Jesus reflected in your character when you are away from Church? When you are at home are you a hellion? Toxic? Hard-to-deal-with? Full of strife and confusion? It is time to do an inner heart check! Christ, all in all, is the hope of glory and the Body of Christ is the vehicle in the Earth that ushers people into Christ by way of the relationships that are fostered outside of the four walls. So, if the Holy Spirit's fruit departs once you leave the church service, and you go home cursing out husband/wife and children, or drinking heavily, being violent tempered, or lazy in the house or in bed, how can people come to know the Jesus you know and be compelled to live for Him? This character does not reflect the Christ you know and will not draw a fly into a trap, let alone an unbelieving spouse.

You have to be mindful of these traits as you are the believing spouse. Once the character of Christ is aligned with your confession, and your heart accepts Jesus as the truth of your life, your character then is able to transform. Your character, given by the Holy Spirit, convicts your spouse because of the holiness flowing through you. The holiness wrought through the Holy Spirit is already sanctifying you both unto salvation. It gives place for your spouse to beckon, *"what must I do to be saved?"* All you have to do is be scripturally equipped to deliver them into the kingdom of God.

### You Must Live Saved Together

Keeping in mind, marriage is for the grown and sexy. You must understand that two grown people become one flesh. In this process of oneness, one spouse cleanses and sanctifies the other spouse's weakness; and this is a two-way street. Marriage is a balancing act. In balancing, Holy Spirit is a real comforting, leading, teaching, and convicting force. Holy Spirit will get you right together in your behaviors, manners, acts, and deeds, as well as heart posture and mindset. Through frustration and conflict, the Holy Spirit will cause you to treat and behave with the character of God towards your spouse. This character will lead you to conflict resolution. Even with intense situations and surging emotions, you must dwell with each other in salvation together. In other words, speak to one another as you both are children of the Most High God and not as though you are angry strangers attempting to get the best of each other. Do not intentionally hurt with your words (cursing, screaming, and belittling).

Moreover, forgive quickly! Forgiveness is the earmark of the righteous! Unforgiveness is the fruit of the unbelieving. Whenever, you have an offense with your spouse, ensure to empty your heart, mind, and memories of the offense. Hanging on to unforgiveness, offense, bitterness, resentment, and hatred will grow and intensify over time and separate you from God. But, guess what? If you have sex with your spouse with undealt issues, and your heart is in a decrepet place against them, you both solidify the offense as one vessel. You both are attaching emotions against one another and binding them to your salvation, which becomes active practicing sin nature. This stumbling block that hampers your personal salvation stifles you and your spouse in walking together and agreeing; and it also makes it difficult to balance Heaven's activity if your soulical environment is not santified. Your soul becomes murky with these weighty natures.

Learn the art of being saved together. Put into practice how to treat one another in heart and action. When you put the character of God into practice and live in the sacrifice of Jesus' blood, whether or not one spouse is flailing in heart and confession, both spouses are covered when one demonstrates the character of God by keeping the command of Jesus is Lord in heart and steadfast confession (which causes transformed behavior). However, when both spouses live saved together, worship together, and enact the fruit of the spirit (the character of God), Heaven and its miracles can become unhinged in your life.

# XIX

## THOU SHALT CREATE PRIORITIES

*For where your treasure is, there will your heart be also.*
### - LUKE 12:34 (NIV)

Oftentimes in marriage, there is the spoouse who spends too much time working outside the house (ie, working jobs, doing ministry, hanging with extended family members or friends), while the other spouse is brooding resentment for feeling last on the list. Working or caring for extended family members or friends is admirable. However, the problem is not what you are doing, but how you are doing it. Both spouses must prioritize the marriage as first. When other nouns (people, places, things, and ideas) come before your spouse, legitimate jealousy has the ability to link into the foundation of your marriage. This legitimate jealousy creates infractions, resentment, and harmful communication within the marriage. Other nouns coming before your spouse is unspoken communication that you treasure something or someone more than you treasure your spouse. Which in turn conveys that this "noun" is where your heart is, and I do not have your heart. This is lawful jealousy because nothing or anyone is supposed to come before your spouse!

This is also where you get the proverbial question, "what is wrong with you?" When you come in the house from these specific nouns and the tension is so thick, you feel as though your spouse is ready to explode and fight about something you have already fought about previously. Your spouse is so annoyed that either you receive back passive aggressive responses (full of attitude) like "nothing" or the completely aggressive response; and then screaming and rude statements ensue. How to avoid this pitfall in your marriage? By honoring and keeping the law of priorities within your marriage.

> *Therefore shall a man leave his father and his mother, and shall cleave unto his wife: and they shall be one flesh.*
> - GENESIS 2:24

You must leave and cleave. This is the foundation of priorities within your marriage: leave and *"forsake all others."* Others may be offended in your obedience to God and the law of marriage. However, allow them to wrestle with your vows and offenses with God. To *"cleave"* is a word of duality in Hebrew and means both to join or adhere with (God and Spouse), and to separate or rend, tear into pieces and divide (from others) at the same time. This is also synonymous with the Hebrew word for "passion" which means, "placement with no exit plans."

On one hand, the spouses must learn to adhere to God and each other, but if the spouse does not come fully into adherence, they will also be cut and divided asunder (emotionally) by cleaving. This is the cut you hear from your spouse, "I feel like I am caught in the middle." Your spouse is literally wrestling with leaving and cleaving and the law of priority about your marriage. And, until the spouse quits the fight against leaving and cleaving and comes into full agreement with, "forsaking all others," their soul will consistently feel the undue false burden of stress. When both spouses understand the nature of cleaving or adhering to one another in agreement, the marriage will come into position. Cleaving or "to cleave" is an action; and it implies a sticking to it [to the end] and sticking with it, which is key to passion." Passion in English and Greek is *pathos,* and it means to be lustful. We are actually speaking of *pathenas* passion. The cleaving that gives birth to passion is not a lustful action. It is the action of holding your spouse close, and nothing is more important than he or she. You are so in agreement, so embraced, so adhered, and so committed to the end that nothing can separate or come between you. Basically, you are so one that others will be cut by this oneness and may misunderstand it. However, this is Godly order, which means both spouses must be in agreement with the prioritization of other nouns. One spouse does not just jump out there and does for mom or dad without both spouses being in honest agreement.

### *Setting Priorities*

*You shall love the Lord your God with all your heart and with all your soul and with all your might.*

— DEUTERONOMY 6:5 (ESV)

### *God:*

Loving God first, being obedient and committed to God, and His will for your life is primary. This should be at the foundation of your marriage. You must have your own prayer life, a word (scriptural study) life, a personal worship life, and then you must have this life together. Being married, you will come to understand that you are in complete need of God to make your marriage work. Additionally, not only should God sovereignly come first in your lives, He must be the center of your lives.

*Beloved, I pray that all may go well with you and that you may be in good health, as it goes well with your soul.*

— III JOHN 1:2 (ESV)

*Self:*

It is equally important for each spouse to not just care for their spouse, but also care for oneself. When spouses are neglectful of themselves, it withers away at the soul and causes emotional, mental, and willful sickness. And, it leads to corrupt behaviors and lack in your finances. Your prosperity is deeply interconnected to the wellness of your soul. Usually, when soul sickness occurs, compulsive behaviors and addictions ensue. The effects are dangerous to the longevity of the marriage as the spouse will become offended, walk in legitimate jealousy, and have a new capacity to bring you to the brink of your emotions blindly, as he/she will lack the language to really deal with the real issues. These are issues that frustrate the spouse and stems from the husbands and wives being neglectful of self. What does that mean? Self-care is not selfishness which is scripturally defined as: *eritheía,* ("mercenary self-seeking") of acting for one's own gain, regardless of the discord (strife) it causes; and it places self-interest, self-seeking, and individualism ahead of what the Lord declares right or what is good for others. When you act independently from your spouse, without agreement and equal submission in situations, you are operating in individualism, which is hell fire dangerous.

> *Now the works of the flesh are evident, which are: adultery, fornication, uncleanness, lewdness, idolatry, sorcery, hatred, contentions, jealousies, outbursts of wrath, selfish ambitions, dissensions, heresies, envy, murders, drunkenness, revelries, and such the like; of which I tell you beforehand, just as I also told you in time past, that those who practice such things will not inherit the kingdom of God. But the fruit of the Spirit is love, joy, peace, longsuffering, kindness, goodness, faithfulness, gentleness, self-control. Against such there is no law. And those who are Christ's have crucified the flesh with its passions and desires. If we live in the Spirit, let you also walk in the Spirit. Let you not become conceited, provoking one another, envying one another.*

> - GALATIANS 5:19-25 (NKJV)

God does not allow you to be an individual person once you marry. Tyler Perry said in the movie *Why Did I Get Married?*—"You give up the I's for the us." There are no longer two but one once you become married. When you contend for individuality, privacy (locked devices, relationships, passwords to accounts and social media accounts) and control, you are in soulical danger of hell. Individuality is violent and contentious in nature. It will contend for personhood at all costs, no matter how your spouse and others may feel. Individuality will stir up strife within the marriage. Because individuality is so rooted in Leviathan and pride, it will blind you of your posture before your spouse and God.

Individuality is selfishness rooted in the core of your spouse's heart and motive. There is eternal punishment according to scripture for this behavior. However, when you are in genuine self-care without selfishness, it looks like a journey walking in agreement to discover yourself in your personal relationship with Christ, education and career endeavors, hobbies, hygiene and appearance, emotional and mental wellness, as well as matters and motives of your heart. Self-care is also caring for your past, present, and future. This level of self-care is unselfish in the fact that it is walking together and agreeing with your spouse that the best version of yourself is the best version you bring to the marriage. For instance, if your wife is ashamed of her body, and has poor self image, she cannot take care of you sexually the way you desire because she is bound. On the contrary, if your wife feels sexy and free, your sex life will unfold as opposed to selfish ambitions where one spouse is unwilling to have sex to control an outcome for a pair of shoes.

*So they are no longer two but one flesh. What therefore God has joined together, let not man separate.*

- Matthew 19:6 (ESV)

### *Spouse:*

Caring for yourself absent of selfishness is innately caring for your spouse and is on the same line as the law of priority. It is also not your priority to work to make your spouse happy. If you are doing this then you are out of alignment with God, and your spouse is your little demi-god. With that being said, you are in some process of becoming one or oneness. No nouns are supposed to come before your spouse or separate you from them physically, emotionally, mentally, conversationally, sexually, willfully, monetarily, intentionally, and passionately. No persons: mother, father, sister, brother, cousins, aunties, uncles, or friends comes before your spouse. No places: jobs, schools, clubs, hang out spots, and the like comes before your spouse. No things: money, bank accounts, credit scores, possessions, and the like comes before your spouse. No ideas: who you think you are, how educated or undereducated you feel, what you feel you have sacrificed and given into the marriage, feelings of unappreciation and unhappiness.

*(Side note: Most spouses in counseling say, "I feel unappreciated," which is a business term—a contracual term; and is really meant to say "underappreciated." When you are in marriage, there is no contract/ business agreement in your feelings. The spouse in the proper context feels "undervalued," which is the actual emotion. Not unappreciated.)*

Moreover, husband's and patriarchal pastors preach that a wife is supposed to just blindly submit to all of his whims and wiles, but scripture gives both spouses heavy duty.

*Submitting yourselves one to another in the fear of God. Wives, submit yourselves unto your own husbands, as unto the Lord. For the husband is the head of the wife, even as Christ is the head of the church: and he is the saviour of the body. Therefore as the church is subject unto Christ, so let the wives be to their own husbands in every thing. Husbands, love your wives, even as Christ also loved the church, and gave himself for it; That he might sanctify and cleanse it with the washing of water by the word, That he might present it to himself a glorious church, not having spot, or wrinkle, or any such thing; but that it should be holy and without blemish. So ought men to love their wives as their own bodies. He that loveth his wife loveth himself. For no man ever yet hated his own flesh; but nourisheth and cherisheth it, even as the Lord the church: For we are members of his body, of his flesh, and of his bones. For this cause shall a man leave his father and mother, and shall be joined unto his wife, and they two shall be one flesh. This is a great mystery: but I speak concerning Christ and the church. Nevertheless let every one of you in particular so love his wife even as himself; and the wife see that she reverence her husband.*

- GALATIANS 5: 21-33

This is a scripture of stealth instructions! Submit to one another or just the wives submit? Here's where we break with false doctrine. Examine that this scripture is speaking as a metaphor of things in natural and spiritual context of marriage. Husbands must be Christlike in order to allow Godly order and submission into his home. Just as Christ Jesus is the head of the church, his character, integrity, and virtue made is obtainable for the wife to fully submit. Additionally, husbands are called to love as Christ loved the Church, meaning He stuck with her through all of her frailty and sacrificed his life for her. In her frailty, abused background, victimized character, and sinful nature, He used and appropriated His own blood and words to restore her back to himself clean of wounds and faults. This marries back to self-care. In order to achieve this kind of love and sacrifice for your wife in accordance to God's standard of husbandry and not one's own ideals, husbands must love themselves. If you do not have a relationship within yourself, you will never receive the power of love's sacrifice that vacates your bride to yourself. On the contrary, she will always fall short in submission because your behaviors demonstrate selfishness (your wants over her necessities).

Wives, do not want instability in love. Instability and insecurity pushes her into the sin nature of doubt and unbelief, which leads to compulsive, combative, and contentious behaviors. Place one another first on your priority list and see how your marriage grows and flourishes. As you place your spouse first, your resources and finances increase. Feed your marriage your time and treasures! Jobs, family, friends, and things will come and go, but your vows are forever.

*Children, obey your parents in the Lord: for this is right. Honor thy father and mother; which is the first commandment with promise; That it may be well with thee, and thou mayest live long on the earth. And, ye fathers, provoke not your children to wrath: but bring them up in the nurture and admonition of the Lord.*
- Ephesians 6:1-4

### *Children:*

Your children are following your marriage in the law of priority. Children are the fruit of your loins, the produce of your marriage, they are not to be placed before the marriage. It's equivalent to asking, "which comes first, the chicken or the egg?" Of course the parents come first. Oftentimes, when women give birth, or adopt, or become a foster mom, her priorities shift because she is a mom. Most women take issue that their babies need to be protected and cared for more than her adult husband who can fend for himself. Mama bear instinct kicks in and everything becomes about caring for her cub. Most mom's even lose sight of caring for herself and begin losing herself to motherhood. Wives must be reminded that she must take time for herself. This can happen when an attentive husband realizes that even though the wife may quit her job or is on leave from work, caring for her cub is intense and his assistance is needed in her tiredness. Do you know what being an attentive husband does? It reveals to his wife that he sees her and cares that she is working hard all day everyday; and he is willing to sacrifice to care for his baby though he too is working hard all day, everyday.

Moreover, when both spouses tend to their children and care for one another it makes parenting and instructing their babies even the more powerful. Scripture instructs that

*"Children, obey your parents…. Honor thy Father and thy Mother, which is the first commandment."* As scripture sets order in children reverencing their origin and obeying parents, this instills order of priority. Notice that in the previous chapter, Ephesians 5:25 deals with the husband and wife order first; however, it flows right into Ephesians 6 that children are next in priority. As children respect their parents, it strengthens the family unit and gives the entire family spiritual authority over the enemy! Ephesians 6 goes into one of the greatest spiritual warfare scriptures:

> *Put on the whole armour of God, that ye may be able to stand against the wiles of the devil. For we wrestle not against flesh and blood, but against principalities, against powers, against the rulers of the darkness of this world, against spiritual wickedness in high places. Wherefore take unto you the whole armour of God, that ye may be able to withstand in the evil day, and having done all, to stand. Stand therefore, having your loins girt about with truth, and having on the breastplate of righteousness; And your feet shod with the preparation of the gospel of peace; Above all, taking the shield of faith, wherewith ye shall be able to quench all the fiery darts of the wicked. And take the helmet of salvation, and the sword of the Spirit, which is the word of God: Praying always with all prayer and supplication in the Spirit, and watching thereunto with all perseverance and supplication for all saints;*
>
> *- EPHESIANS 6:11-28*

Authority is given by way of submission to authority and by setting order and priorities. The relationship between spiritual authority, order, and submission are intimately woven together! Without one or the other, you will not operate in authority in the spirit realm and shift demonic opposition away from your home, which is deeply important! Why is spiritual authority important in your home? First, when instructing and raising your children, their honor should clothe you in the spirit as you cover them spiritually and naturally. Second, dad's, as you clothe your children with love and balance of instruction in the spirit of wisdom, and discipline them in love with intentionality, you are conveying to your children and empowering them to love Father God. Clothing your children in this way conveys the truth of the nature of Father God.

Children need to know that mom and dad come first to one another and love one another. It imparts to them security. Security in turn grows them in intellect, spirit, and confidence, but this happens when they know innately that there is no dividing mom and dad or manipulating mom and dad (asking mom for something does not get the proper response). Mom telling the child to go and ask dad will yield the proper result. Children who violate this order clothes the parents in dishonor, divides the house asunder, and causes the parents to lose spiritual authority because the children have become the priority.

*Let thy garments be always white; and let thy head lack no ointment. Live joyfully with the wife whom thou lovest all the days of the life of thy vanity, which he hath given thee under the sun, all the days of thy vanity: for that is thy portion in this life, and in thy labour which thou takest under the sun. Whatsoever thy hand findeth to do, do it with thy might; for there is no work, nor device, nor knowledge, nor wisdom, in the grave, whither thou goest. I returned, and saw under the sun, that the race is not to the swift, nor the battle to the strong, neither yet bread to the wise, nor yet riches to men of understanding, nor yet feavyour to men of skill; but time and chance happeneth to them all.*

- ECCLESIASTES 9:8-12

### *Work and/or Education:*

This scripture sets order for work. *"Let your garments always be white and do not let your head lack any ointment."* Which means to always live a blameless, holy, and anointed lifestyle. Never lack nor slack in your relationship with God, and never slack in anointing. Then, *"live joyfully with the wife whom you love all the days of your life."* After the Godly order is established by stating *"be a vessel anointed and holy,"* it is followed by, *"enjoy your wife."* Finally, King Solomon begins to speak about the order in the Law of Priority that is placed after God and spouse. Notice King Solomon gives sobering realities about working and amassing wealth. He says that it is nothing more than vanity, and eventually all are subject to end in death, so learn to enjoy your life now. You are given only an allotted amount of time and limited chances!

> *For if someone does not know how to manage his own household, how will he care for God's church?*
>
> — I TIMOTHY 3:5 (NLT).

## *Church:*

Primarily, the family unit was birthed first before the Church in God's creation of institutions and family mechanisms. The first family is observed in the Book of Genesis, and the Church was brought forth in the Acts of the Apostles. Men are given one wife just as Jesus was given a wife—*the Church*. You are not to care for another man's wife more than one's own. The mindset that the Church and the family comes first is perverted thinking. The woman or man you vowed your life to is the first in the order of priority. Always be certain that home is completely handled in every way, i.e. physical energy, being mentally and emotionally present, financially strong, and the health and wellbeing of all in the home are in peace. No one likes to do ministry knowing their spouse is at home or in the presence of other saints resenting the work of the ministry. The spouse is in legitimate jealousy of the ministry, and hell is breaking loose in the home when the doors are closed as a result. Moreover, when your priorities are perverted, it decreases your spiritual authority.

> *So they are no longer two but one flesh. What therefore God has joined together, let not man separate.*
>
> — MATTHEW 19:6 (ESV)

### *Extended Family Members and Friends:*
**(can be interchangeable with church given the circumstances)**

Extended family members are grouped into parents, grandparents, aunts, uncles, siblings, and cousins. Once you are married you have become one unit and are now a foundation for a nuclear family. This is the elemental beginning of your family. Mom and Dad and their desires come after your spouse. Do not allow yourself to be the person to put asunder or separate your marriage because you are not putting your priorities into perspective.

Additionally, do not allow those outside of your marriage in your extended family to put your marriage asunder. Do not allow your spouse to be uncovered by extended family members. Do not let them speak negatively about your spouse without asserting your truth. Command respect for your spouse, and stand in your being one in this position. Many times, a spouse will feel uncomfortable around extended family members and vent about this uncomfortability. The opposite spouse will feel resentful and unaccepted by the spouse because he/she may feel that if you do not accept their family then it is an automatic assumption of negative feelings and non-acceptance of the spouse because of his/her background. Do not accept the lies of the enemy. Minister to one another and bind yourselves to each other. Command respect from both extended families by disallowing negative statements and behaviors. Stand as a unit in agreement that those who speak against or behave negatively against your union will be escorted away from both spouses because no one is to separate you in ideals, deeds, words, actions, and behaviors. If one spouse is not accepted, both spouses must stand as a unit and solidify your union away from those that clothe it with dishonor causing disparity in the home.

In addition, friends that cause friction in the home are not to be friends with either spouse. Friends must honor the marriage and both spouses. Moreover, both spouses must agree upon friendships that are wise, have a healthy outlook on marital situations, and can still love both spouses without bias. They must also be prayerful, loving, and display feelings of honor towards the marriage and both spouses. If one spouse does not like this particular friend, the friendship cannot persist. On the other hand, if the friend does not like your spouse, the friendship cannot persist. Friends must respect both spouses and honor the totality of the marriage.

*And this is my prayer: that your love may abound more and more in knowledge and depth of insight, so that you may be able to discern what is best and may be pure and blameless for the day of Christ, filled with the fruit of righteousness that comes through Jesus Christ—to the glory and praise of God.*
                                                                    - Philippians 1:9-11(NIV)

## *Hobbies:*

Hobbies are a funny thing. They can be fun and time consuming, but they also keep you mentally sharp and emotionally healthy. Hobbies allow for spouses to decompress; and for the introverted spouse, it gives them much needed quiet time to recuperate. Hobbies come in the form of building or repairing, reading, video games, movies, music (playing or listening), driving, talking on the phone, social media, and other activities that calms and releases tranquility. However, some hobbies are sinful and obsessive with a compulsive and addictive nature. Those kinds of hobbies are harmful to your spouse and marriage.

Moreover, hobbies out of priority cause legitimate jealousy in your spouse. For instance, husbands that love to play video games too much or for too long and the wife is competing for your affection and attention has legitmate jealousy. Here is another instance: a wife is glued to her phone chatting, texting, playing games, and on social media all day. However, when the husband comes to have a conversation, the wife is attentively looking at her phone instead of her husband, which causes him to check out in return for feelings of neglect *(Checking out is a form of legitimate jealousy.)*. Both hobbies are outside of the law of priority because an unspoken communication of unimportance was subliminally communicated to the opposite spouse even though it seemed harmless and sinless in nature. Hobbies must be prioritised and agreed upon with both spouses. How much time is fine to be spent on the hobby? What time is "your time?" And giving your spouse an invitation to join you inside of your hobby also involves them in your world!

# XX

## Thou Shalt Maintain Pursuit In Your Marriage

True love will chase you down, tie you up, and make you want to submit. If you have ever been in love, you know that while you are in passion, there is no limit to what you can and will do. Girls float around with smiles on their faces. Men are so full that love songs fill their lips. The indescribable feelings take root in the soul and intoxicate the bearer. There are no bad days, just days that make you fall deeper in love. Even the things that are not supposed to be attractive become features that radically charge the heart. Your ears hear frequencies that normally could not be heard. Every touch is stronger and more tantalizing than the last. The impulsive response of nature's tendency to chase another blindly into love is crazy. However, you do it and you do it gladly. There is no feeling in the world quite like running after someone and not truly knowing exactly where you two will end. Will the chaser catch the pursuit?? Will both lovers fall into a cloud of darkness and never touch the love they both sought after?

Every good action movie involves a chase scene. Every good horror film involve someone being chased and killed. Every good romance involves a lover enduring, beating the odds, winning a heart, and chasing the love of a life time. If its gonna be good then there will be a chase. NO CHASE MEANS NO PASSION. There is no getting around this principle. The truth is that everyone wants to be chased. This definitely includes men. On the contrary, to popular belief, men need to be not only respected but loved as well. Men need to know that the woman that he has invested into wants to invest into him as well. The goal of the relationship is that both the man and the woman pursue one another fervently. This never ending pursuit leads to showing us how God loves us. You never want your relationships to resemble the world in all of its attributes. Why? Well when you love like the world, you get a worldly out come. For example, the world will love you today, hate you tomorrow, and be quite fickle. God does not want your marriage fickle and unstable. God designed it to be strong and enthusiastically loving.

Pursuing your mate is the hidden key for a successful marriage. Unfortunately, you don't always pursue your mates. Oftentimes, you overlook this concept and look to prefer and pursue selfish ideals. There are three reasons why spouses don't pursue one another. The first reason is that there has been a traumatic experience that has now changed your spouses "would-be" loving behavior. Trauma can be introduced to an individual as a child, and the unfavorable effects of trauma are wide reaching. However, these things can stem from abusive parents, parental rejection, negative upbringing, and sexual abuse, including molestation and rape, and parental or familial abandonment.

The second reason is self-protection. At this point, one spouse has deemed the relationship to be unsafe. This could be because of a trust that was broken previously or presently. Either way, a note is placed in the mind of the fearful spouse that states, "do not trust this person;" or "this relationship is not real;" or " they will not love me anymore once they get what they want." Everytime the fearful spouse is supposed to pursue with nice words, they tend not to have the right words to say. Everytime the fearful spouse is suppose to pursue with actions that demonstrate love and appreciation, those actions fall very flat. Sex is fleeting and rare to those that have a spouse who is in the pain of self-protection. They can't get those notes or voices out of their heads. It is the sound of a screaming individual. Don't chase him! Dont have sex with him! Don't give him a hug! Don't express warmth because the moment you open up he will fail you. The moment you open up he will break your heart. If you stay closed you will never have to have the catastrophe of being open to love. Unfortunately, the person that is in self-protection will truly never have love. All they can hold on to at night is a pillow of fear, self pity, and deception. True love requires trust. True love requires letting go of control. True love requires pursuit.

The third reason why a person does not pursue is because the relationship has lost priority. It is simply not a priority to one spouse or both spouses. When the marriage loses its priority or shifts position and priority, the relationship is in danger. For example, we know that good priorities are putting God first, second the husband and wife, then the children come third, your job or way that provides money comes fourth, fifth is your church (going to worship, volunteering, and serving), then your extended family, and finally your hobbies and recreation. When one of these priorities shifts out of order, it leads to each and every other priority being dysfunctional, mismanaged, and abused. For example, when a man chooses to work 18 hours a day, every day, he puts the job in front of his wife, family, and "God!" This is dysfunctional and will not work according to God's principles. How can that man be present for his children? How can that man be present for his wife? More importantly, how can that man worship God? The truth is that he doesn't and will not worship God, nor will he be present and available to his wife and children.

You need your priorities and passions to align in order to pursue. These unlawful priorities create unlawful pursuit. With unlawful pursuit comes chasing everything else except for your spouse, which is a pseudospouse; and your spouse should always be the object of your chase.

### The Perverse Cleave

Cleaving is absolutely biblical and essential to having an UNBreakable Marriage. However, Satan wants to destroy or break apart everything. Anything of value will be attacked or tampered with by satanic thoughts and behaviors. Your marriage is valuable. Satan installs perversion to twist the truth out of our relationships. The truth is that husbands and wives are to cleave to one another. Perversion is when parents cleave to their children's marriage. Parents are a killer to many marriages. Especially perverse parents. These are the parents who feel like they have the right to involve themselves deeply in the life of their children's marriage. Parents that do this steal the identity of their child's marriage. This happens when parents have too much of a say in their child's marriage, such as constant opinions about what they would do, constant insults about how the child parents their children, or constant accusations and pitting one child over the other. Parents who are pushy even after boundaries have been made are wrong.

Typically, the parent gives selfish reasons for this aggressive behavior. For example, a mom may say, "I was here first," or a dad may say, "Im just trying to help. There is a such thing as TOO MUCH HELP. This type of entanglement creates a river of hate for at least one of the spouses and embittered rage in the soul of the marriage. Friends who have feelings for one spouse or were in relationship before the marriage, feel that their positon is before or higher than the marriage. Jealousy is birthed into existence when the spouse stands up for the marriage. Placing this friend back in their place of being behind or lower in priority is how you undo the perverse ownership of a friend. Contentious feelings may flare up, but breaking the hold of this friend from the marriage is the only way for the marriage to survive. If a spouse teams up with the friend, he or she is actually separating their own marriage.

Once married you are not allowed to jump and switch teams. The person you married must be the number one priority over all other friends physically, emotionally, mentally, and in every other sense of life. If your attachment to an outside friend outweighs your wife or husband, you are in a perverse cleave. End it immediately, and save your marriage. The job and the work wife/husband are very capable of introducing hell into your life. Overworking and chasing money has hurt many. Some would say, "I'm just going to work because we need the money;" or "I am working for you (us)." The truth is that overworking is simply a cover up. Marriage to your job is not the will of God. And your spouse does not deserve to be placed beneath the demands of a job that could fire you at any time. The work wife/husband is a derivitive of this deceptive lifestyle. Giving a coworker all your emotional energy, secrets, and sexual ideals is prohibited. If a coworker is doing this then they are breaking boundaries. From this, emotional and physical affairs are born. Because you feel you have a deep connection and chemistry with a person does not give you the right to betray your marriage. Because this work spouse makes you feel excitement, spice, and needed does not open the door to indulgence. Early to work, late getting home, hanging out and grabbing drinks with the opposite sex under the guise of work, consistent indecent propositions, and conversations that touch the deep line of ecstacy—if this is happening, then the marriage is being intruded upon. Defend your marriage from enemies far and near, outside and inside, and perverse psuedo spouses.

### You can't touch this!

When I was younger I used to watch cartoons. This cartoon in particular had a road runner and a coyote. The coyote would determine in his heart and mind that he was gonna catch and have the roadrunner for dinner. The roadrunner always had different plans. This made for a sort of cat and mouse type of story line. The road runner had some special abilities and was super fast. The coyote was not fast, but he was innovative. The coyote knew he could never match the roadrunner's speed so he would try traps, rocket boosters, and any mechanical contraption he could think of to get the job done of catching the roadrunner.

Coyote never really caught the roadrunner; and when he did, it was only for a couple moments. Then the magical illusive powers of the roadrunner always got him free and running 100 mph. No matter what coyote tried, he just could never really capture and keep the road runner. The fact that coyote's victories were always short lived is sad. However, it was really one of the most entertaining cartoons I've seen. Many marriages look exactly like Roadrunner and Coyote episodes. A husband is taking a wife out on the town. They are having a great time. In fact, this is the best time they have had since last week. He reaches out to hold hands, she doesn't notice. He says really nice things to her. She smiles, but she never has good words to say back to him. The husband is determined to give his all to his wife. She is having a great time, but she does not understand what is actually happening in the marriage. He is simply trying to touch her heart, but there is an invisible force field around it.

A wife wakes up and kisses her husband good morning. He grumpily replies leave me alone. She takes no offense and simply rolls out of bed to start cooking breakfast. Scrambled eggs, hashbrowns, turkey bacon (his favorite), and pancakes cooked to perfection are sat on the table. Wife takes time to pour apple juice into his cup as husband rushes down stairs to take a piece of bacon and run out the door. She sits at the table wondering why he can't see her and all she is doing. She then determines in herself that she will get him to notice her, so she calls off of work to cleanse everything and decides to make perch with a side of broccoli to perfection. Then she lights candles to set a mood right before he pulls into the driveway. He sits in the car breathing heavy slightly annoyed by the day. She says to herself, "I got something for all that stress. I'm gonna take his breath away tonight." He finally comes in. She tries to greet him, but he gives her a quick peck and goes into the bathroom for an hour. She reheats the food and sits at the table. He comes out to find an excellent smelling meal on the table. He looks down and tells her he has already eaten and is now tired and ready for bed. She says, "can we talk? How was your day?" He says "it was long, and I'm tired." As he lays in the bed, she sits at the kitchen table wondering what is happening. She is doing everything, but nothing is good enough. She chases him but can't catch his heart.....

In both cases someone is giving chase and someone is running away. If this type of relationship continues, discouragement will set in and take root in the relationship. Rejection hurts. Consistent discouragement to pursue your spouse breaks the will of the marriage. It steals the love and passion from your marriage. So consider, if you are fighting for love and trying to feel those feelings of desire again, think about where the rejection and discouragement is coming from. It may be coming from YOUR MOUTH OR YOUR

NON-VERBAL/BODY COMMUNICATION. Repent! Say you are sorry, and change your language. If you don't, then you will be the reason and center of pride and abuse that breaks everything. Eventually the spouse with the most injury will look for ways to leave. Most start leaving mentally first, then emotionally, and finally physically. This is natural for most people.

To resolve the Road-runner and Coyote issues, it requires that at least one spouse retraces the hurtful places of rejection. In this retracing process, you will find that you have to do some hard forgiveness of your spouse, forgiveness for the traumatic effects of your past, and forgiveness for yourself. Some of the stuff that has happened in your marriage may have been from a get back spirit, but I believe that most of the trespasses are not intentional. If you believe the same, then its beneficial to forgive, forget, let it go, and learn to love. Love is the process of acceptance of the good, bad, and oneness with no bad intentions for your spouse. Love overwhelms the idea that "he may hurt me again." Love conquers the thoughts of "I dont want to deal with her nasty attitude anymore" and adds more love to touch her heart. Love sees what isn't easily seen. Love makes treasure in the midst of trash. Love will bring compassion and gratefulness into your marriage. The spirit of entitlement is a prideful killer. You are not entitled to perfection. Breaking the rejection requires you to break covetousness and lust, and simply love the one you are with. Love all of their perfections and misinterpreted perfections. Real love gets you back on track.

Dr. Jermael & Dr. Carrie's

# UNBREAKABLE BONUS

# BONUS #1

## THOU SHALT DATE

*Come, my beloved, let you go forth into the field; let you lodge in the villages. Let you get up early to the vineyards; let you see if the vine flourish, whether the tender grape appear, and the pomegranates bud forth: there will I give thee my loves. The mandrakes give a smell, and at your gates are all manner of pleasant fruits, new and old, which I have laid up for thee, O my beloved.*

### - SONGS OF SOLOMON 7:11-13

It is imperative that married couples have a routined date night! Just because you have hooked them in and captured them for the rest of your life does not mean you can be cheap and lazy! No matter what your budget is, date! Dating your spouse allows you to retool your marriage. Dating your spouse allows you both to rediscover each other without the stressors of the world, i.e. career, children, grandchildren, volunteering, or opportunities that get in the way. Dating allows you to reconnect to one another. By dating, you both are allowed to simply be yourselves to laugh and play with each other. Dating re-establishes your bond and brings you into intimacy. Be creative as you once were when you dated before your marriage.

Examples of date night ideas are going to the opera, orchestra, travelling, playing, movies, dinner, breakfast, coffee, paintballing, walking the mall, gala, drive in movies, movie night at home, cuddling in your loving bed and watching television, or sitting up for hours to dream together. As you see, all of those date night ideas are a range of budgets, so there is no reason why you should not date. Moreover, when your children or grandchildren are with you, it is no longer date night. You are now having "family night." If your children are always with you when you and your spouse venture out together, then you have never had a date night. You have always had family night. Now it is time to re-affirm your bond without your children. Get a babysitter, send the grandbabies back to their parents, and have your time together!

### Non-negotiables During Date Night

Date night must come with non-negotiables! You and your spouse must have one another's undivided attention. Do not abruptly end conversations with your spouse to answer the phone, half-listen to your spouse due to sports, play games on your devices, or be absent during your dating duties. This sends a nonverbal message to your spouse that they are not as valuable as other ideas and objectives. This type of communication can offend or choke out intimacy between you and your spouse. Meaning, you must be present! Give one hundred percent on date night to your spouse! Give them all of your attention, conversation, jokes, laughs, hand holding, flirtation, memories, and visions for the future together! This is your chance to leave work, children, parents, and family issues out of your life, and embrace one another!

Moreover, we must acknowledge what every marriage has been through, which are date nights that begin with a fight of some kind when attempting to spend time together. Date night is not for arguments and fighting! It is about reconnecting, and any issue that prevents reconnection and rediscovery is not for your planned date night, no matter the emotional upheaval. Learn to make date night a peaceful and fun night to like and love on your spouse. Another non-negotiable on date night is sex. Life moves so fast.

Oftentimes, couples in this era are so busy that if sex is not scheduled, it is missed. A lack of sex is a marriage killer. Lack of sex is one of the top three reasons why marriages end in divorce court. So, on date night, make it about him or make it about her; and better yet, make it about each other to bring love, passion, and pleasure to satisfy the needs of both spouses. Retool yourself and explore your spouses body on datenight. Have honest sex and locate what is pleasurable and what is not pleasurable in your marriage bed. Perfect it, and bring one another to Heaven. As you place these principles into position in your marriage, both spouses will become so excited about date night because peace and love comes so naturally. You both get to enjoy the ever growing chemistry and presence of God with your spouse! Bonus, you get to draw closer together intimately, grow, and have good sex!

# BONUS #2

## THOU SHALT HAVE GOOD SEX

*Marriage is honourable in all, and the bed undefiled:*
**- HEBREWS 13:4**

The institution of marriage is honourable in all things and should be honored by all. Those who are outside of marriages, i.e., extended family, friends, and others must understand that God has placed honor on marriage, and it is not to be taken lightly. Society needs to get back to the fear of God in respecting other marriages, as well as equal spousal respect for the union they have vowed to maintain. Innately, the marriage bed is a place of healing, love, communication, creation, intimacy, truth, reality, connection, redemption, and passion. Contrary to popular belief God meets you in your bed(room). Moreover, the marriage bed is not a place of lust and unbridled secularism (a place just to get proverbially freaky). Because there is bodily nakedness, emotional nakedness, and mental nakedness in the marriage bed, it leads you to believe that there must be complete truth in the marriage bed. Truth alone is found in Christ, which draws the imprint of God into the marriage bed. When deception is found there, it riddles everything outside of the marriage bed with the spirit of lies and deception.

### Do not tolerate the false prophetess Jezebel

Jezebel attempts to usurp your authority through sexuality, control, and witchcraft. This is a diabolical scheme that spouses attempt to hold over the sexual prowess of the other to gain selfish desires. Holding out on your spouse to prove a point, argue, or gain an advantage in a situation is Jezebelic control and witchcraft operating in sexuality. Jezebel, who called herself a prophetess, was a priestess of Baal and Ashtoreth. Baal was the son of Ashtoreth and El. Baal killed his father El and took his mother, Ashtoreth, as his mistress. Perverted? Almost! The followers of Baal and Astoreth worshippers would then commit sexual acts to simulate what they desired the gods (Baal and Astoreth) to do to create their outcomes. The heightening of sexual desire via lust or perversion and/orgasm or lack of orgasm would gain an advantage or outcome for their "harvests." Now perverse? Yes! This is the self same spirit that plagues marriages today. Witholding sex, sexual overdrive (hypersexuality), and a lack of sexual desire (hyposexuality) are selfish to produce an outcome (harvest), whether preceived good or bad. Holy scriptures instructs the saints otherwise:

> Let the husband render unto the wife due benevolence: and likewise also the wife unto the husband. The wife hath not power of her own body, but the husband: and likewise also the husband hath not power of his own body, but the wife. Defraud ye not one the other, except it be with consent for a time, that ye may give yourselves to fasting and prayer; and come together again, that Satan tempt you not for your incontinency.

> - 1 CORINTHIANS 7:3-4

Meaning, we are to give due benevolence. The Greek word for benevolence is *eunoia*, meaning good-will, kindliness; enthusiasm. In essence, give your spouse the sex that you both desire with enthusiasm, excitement, passion, and desire. Do not give your spouse your traumas, rapes, molestations, inappropiate touches, past experiences, body shame, and past sexual relationships (whether comparison to good sex or bad sex experiences). Moreover, do not give your spouse the crumbs of your day (i.e., the fact that you have cooked, cleaned, worked, and are now too tired for sexual activities).

### *Soul Honesty In the Marriage Bed*

Sexuality is the total person. This is why the devil fights sexuality so intensely with shame and confusion. The enemy knows this is the place of great productivity and generational blessings. Therefore, he wraps ungodly rules and feelings around the marriage bed. Firstly, learn to be free! No one can tell any particular marriage what they can and cannot do because scripture brings definitive outlines around the marriage bed, which includes sex acts, when you can and cannot have sex, or even having sex around the period.

Bring truth into your marriage bed. Define what is good sex for you! Do not get into the marriage bed faking orgasms, overacting, and being phony if that is not your natural behavior. Lying about orgasming breeds lying spirits to permeate the entire life of the marriage. Faking in the marriage bed is also a breeding ground for distrust. Be honest. Do you honestly like what is happening. Both spouses must exercise patience in learning ecstasy of your unique sexuality. What touches work for you? What pressure of touch? Do you have issues with nakedness? Do you need something extra to assist you in moving into the mindset of lovemaking? Do you take sex too seriously? Can both spouses be free? Will you allow your spouse to be free in sex?

In order to get to this level of freedom in your marriage bed you must first remove all images. All images of pornography, past experiences, and romance movies bring an imagination to what one thinks sex is supposed to be. You are not married to or having sex with those images. You are with your spouse, the real person, and their real expression of love towards you! You cannot bring your past into your bed. Leave them and those images in the past! Do not add godless items into your marriage bed, such as vibrators, extra individuals, and fruitless objects. Moreover, if your spouse vetoes a specific sex act, then that sex act is off limits until you both revisit the idea and both agree. Defiling your marriage bed occurs when both spouses do not agree on sex acts, when there are extra individuals in the marriage bed, when you sexually reject your spouse without probable reason, and when you involve fruitless and godless objects.

### Good Sex Permeates All of your Senses

Yes! Yes! Yes! Good sex is the command of the Lord! God wants you to have good sex. Good sex is apart of God's plan for your union. Anyone that is married or unmarried that says differently has simply been out of the will of God. These people just dont know what it is like to have good sex so they could never tell you about it. It's like a child that reaches for the moon at night believing that they will never touch it because this has always been their experience. Fools keep having experiences that leave them short of the mark. You can get older but that does not mean that you have taken in the wisdom from the experiences life has given you. Since you are available to have sex, why not have good sex?

Good sex is subjective to the givers and receivers. There is a secret that everyone is holding in their heart. Good sex is like the saying, "beauty is in the eye of the beholder." However, everyone is holding the same eyes. "Love is blind, but your neighbors are not!" Everyone knows what they want, but they may not know how to put language to it.

God made good sex to permeate all of the senses He has given you.

*Sight* - what you are seeing, how you are perceiving your spouse, and turning on the sight of your aroused or unaroused spouse.

*Hearing* - what you hear before sex, the words you speak that build life and substance in your spouse during the day. You are aroused to the words and sounds that come from your spouse.

*Touch* - kissing, holding, cuddling, embracing, subtle grabs, and gentle touches whether aroused or unaroused assists in taking your spouse into your senses. Touching is a way of allowing your tactile senses to capture and remember your spouse. Touch also identifies and sets you apart from everyone else around your spouse.

*Smell* - Whether coming home to the smell of a hearty meal, desserts baking in the oven, or the smell of candles burning—a powerful component of human sexuality is smell. Whether one's own natural body chemistry smell or perfumes and colognes, men and women alike are driven by scent. Having good hygiene and allowing your natural body scent to be cleansed, fortifies your spouse's senses and draws them into their most primal nature. In addition, perfumes and colognes that are a known turn on for your spouse, touches them in an instinctual nature and creates an atmosphere for the desire of your appetites to rise.

*Taste* - Tantalize your spouse with good foods, drinks, and kisses! Just be mindful for a more expansive experience before sex. Please do go to the bathroom, and prepare while there. Do not overeat or overdrink as these matters dampen the moment!

*Spirit* - Making love reinforces and strengthens your marital covenant, vows, and cements your being one in the spiritual realm. Naturally, making love is deeply impacted by intercourse in the spiritual realm; and feelings of love, affection, warmth, closeness, adoration, and fondness ensue. Moreover, you both want to involve Holy Spirit because Holy Spirit is ever present. Acknowledge Holy Spirit's presence as Holy Spirit will lead you into all truth and teach you what satisfies your spouse, and what does not excite your spouse. You can do this by praying together before you enter into making love to set the atmosphere. During sex, worship God together!

*Mind* - Be of one mind and in agreement with the sexual acts that you indulge in. Both spouses should also be in agreement and in one mind on the purpose of the sexual encounters without agendas (trying to master your spouse into a position for selfish ambitions and opportunities), and that you are there for love, connection, bonding, drawing closer in intimacy, and both are working towards each other's pleasure. There is not just one spouse's pleasure, but there is an opportunity for both spouses to be pleasured and taken to Heaven together! Do not limit your capacity for pleasure and oneness with your spouse, or rob them of you experiencing pleasure by worrying, thinking too much, and focusing on other things such as children, bills, jobs, responsibilities; or "I am just getting them off." Make it about your marriage and you cementing your bond by satisfying one another's needs, wants, and desires!

*Will* - Will is defined by Webster's Dictionary as (1) "English: expressing inevitable events" (2) Hebrew: Noun – katon pattern, masculine meaning, "desire, intent, will." When the hour arises for sexual activity, there must be shared willingness, desire, intention, and a certain mindfulness that this shared time is inevitable and definitive. One spouse should not do all of the sexual pursuit. There must be a certain inevitability of equal pursuit in your sex lifeknowing that your body is no longer yours and your spouse's body is no longer theirs, but each body is equally desirous of the other. This intentional desire and love must be expressed in a way that is honorable, intense, and passionate. However, it starts with equal honesty in your desires and motivations.

***Emotions*** - The joy of sex, the laughter before sexual activity and laughter together during sexual activity. If you have never laughed during sex, what are you waiting for? Sex, should not be this lean pumping moment but an experience of happiness, fun, and shared pleasure. Pleasure brings laughter. It is not that you are laughing at your spouse in your most vulnerable moment but laughing with your spouse and being in the moment together. Next, your emotions should attempt to capture love as it is all encompassing. Love is: a feeling, a mindset, a choice, an intentional decision, an act (whether expressing in the most beautiful way in sex or in gifts, acts of service, words of affirmation, spending quality time or physical touch [5 Love Languages by Gary Chapman]).

***Heart*** - Heart in Greek is *kardia* and is defined as intentional intensity. Focus mututally on all of the accutroments of good sex: love, honor, humor, respect, cementing your vows, and reaffirming spouse's primary position in your life. Good Sex is not shameful or taboo. Good sex is the bonding agent of your marriage and identity as one. Good sex assists into oneness and cement of your vows. Enjoy good sex together and never take good sex for granted.

# BONUS #3

## THOU SHALT NOT DEPEND ON THY SPOUSE TO MAKE YOU HAPPY

*Be strong and courageous, all you who hope in the LORD.*
**- PSALM 31:24**

A major complaint within a lot of marriages is, "I work hard to make him/her happy, and it seems like nothing I do can achieve that." Let's take the spirit of deception out of marriage. Are you ready? It is not your responsibility to make your husband or wife happy! It is each of your responsibility to be strong in the Lord and exercise the joy of the Lord which is your strength. You alone are responsible for your own emotions. You are responsible for your own happiness. The moment you decide to be someone's happiness, you have decided to control your spouse. You may have done this unintentionally. If so, you are wrong and out of your right position in the marriage. This is similar to having a dislocated bone. It's extremely painful, and it cannot hold weight. The moment you choose to place weight on the dislocated bone, there is a strong chance that you will shatter or break that bone; and unfortunately, everything attached to that bone is now negatively affected.

Please listen. You are not alone in this. Everyone has done it. You wanted so badly to make your loved one happy just like they do on the TV shows or the romantic movies. When you are in love, you will do anything to make them happy. Being someone's happiness or someone's peace is not

Godly. It is Satanic in nature because it releases dysfunction and disorder into the relationship. This type of positioning in a relationship actually rips the other person from God and subscribes them to lean on you for the very things they should be leaning on God for.

> *May the God of hope fill you with all joy and peace in believing, so that by the power of the Holy Spirit you may abound in hope.*
>
> - ROMANS 15:13 (ESV)

You cannot be God nor the Holy Spirit. You can only be you.

You must remember that emotions are a very temporary thing: happy today and upset tomorrow. However, the joy of the Lord is a nutrient of the Fruit of the Spirit which points to two truths: (1) Joy is controlled by Holy Spirit and cannot be manufactured into the emotions. It can only be experienced as a constant state of being:

> *But the fruit of the Spirit is love, joy, peace, longsuffering, gentleness, goodness, faith, Meekness, temperance: against such there is no law.*
>
> - GALATIANS 5:22-23

And, as you walk in this constant state, you can remain joyful despite bad things happening that will attempt to steal your joy away. (2) Happiness is temporal and joy is everlasting. Happiness is fleeting because its foundation is not a stabilizing force. Emotions are a part of your soulical realm. It is the chemical reaction of God breathing His Spirit into formed dirt. God's spirit is so powerful that when He breathed in Adam's nostrils he became a living soul. God's creative force of wind activated and animated Adam (formed inanimate dirt) into life. Man, formed by dirt (what you can see), comes to life by God's creative wind (what you cannot see). And this life force that you can perceive by feeling or experience, whether emotional, mindforce, heart intentions, or will power (the middle ground), is volatile and unstable.

The soul of a man has to experience salvation for stability. He has to be placed under the subjection of the Holy Spirit to remain in character with the Fruit of the Spirit (the divine character of God). In understanding where emotions come from and Who governs them, it is up to your spouse to govern their soul's posture before God. This is why buying things, giving the best sex, cooking a good comfort meal, being controlled, or controlling will not make your spouse happy. Attempting to control outcomes in your household by lying about your truths and keeping real heart truths secret from your spouse because, "I don't want to hurt you," does not make your spouse happy either. In contrast, this hurts you, your marriage, and your spouse more. Each spouse must understand their personal role in happiness. You cannot turn your spouse into your god to create an idolatrous environment for your personal happiness. Happiness is yours to own. Just like your unhappiness is yours to own. It is not your spouse or marriage's responsibility to create your happy views for life. Just like it is not your marriage that makes you happy or unhappy. Unhappiness is a fallen nature (fleshly outlook on life and marriage). When a spouse says, "I am unhappy," they are actually signaling the belief that "My life in Christ is ruined, and I am blaming you (spouse). I am creating this marriage for my personal unhappiness." Reading what is being communicated spiritually and soulically reads selfishness. Joy on the other hand is a godly character standard. Unhappiness and happiness is a fleshly (fallen nature and sinful) standard, and nothing good dwells in happiness and unhappiness. Happiness is only good when it is stimulated through the joy of Holy Spirit. Having the complete fruit of the Spirit manifesting in your life to hedge your hapiness into *"righteousness, joy, and peace in the Holy Ghost."*

If you loved *The Unbreakable Marriage: 20 Commands of Marriage*, purchase our next book...

# THE UNBREAKABLE MARRIAGE: BOUDOIR EDITION

...where you will learn how to have the best sex of your life!

# CONNECT WITH US!

For speaking engagements, counseling sessions, and book readings, contact us at:

**Dr. Jermael and Dr. Carrie Anthony**
611 W. 63rd Street
P.O. Box 21575
Chicago, IL 60621
(312) 890-8136

## FOLLOW US ON SOCIAL MEDIA

**FACEBOOK:** Drs. Jermael and Carrie
**INSTAGRAM:** Drsjermael_and_carrie
**CLUBHOUSE:** Drs. J and C

## EMAIL
kingdomathand@gmail.com

Made in the USA
Monee, IL
05 May 2022